A Sunday Reader

Illustrated Narratives from the

OLD AND NEW TESTAMENTS

CAIN AND ABEL.   SIR FREDK. LEIGHTON, P.R.A., DELᴛ.

A Sunday Reader

Illustrated Narratives from the
OLD AND NEW TESTAMENTS

Edited by Aley Fox

DOVER PUBLICATIONS, INC.
Mineola, New York

Bibliographical Note

This Dover edition, first published in 2015, is an unabridged republication of the work originally published by Edwin Dalton, London, c. 1910, under the title *Art Pictures from the Old Testament and Our Lord's Parables / A Series of One Hundred and Seventeen Illustrations.*

Library of Congress Cataloging-in-Publication Data

Art pictures from the Old Testament.
    A Sunday reader : Illustrated narratives from the Old and New Testaments / Edited by Aley Fox.
        pages cm
    "This Dover edition, first published in 2015, is an unabridged republication of the work originally published by Edwin Dalton, London, c. 1910, under the title *Art Pictures from the Old Testament and Our Lord's Parables / A Series of One Hundred and Seventeen Illustrations.*"
    ISBN-13: 978-0-486-79480-8
    ISBN-10: 0-486-79480-6
    1. Bible. Old Testament—Illustrations. I. Fox, Aley. II. Dalton, Edwin, 1845–1925. III. Title.
NE958.3.G7A78 2015
769'.484—dc23   2014040694

Manufactured in the United States by Courier Corporation
79480601   2015
www.doverpublications.com

ART PICTURES

FROM THE

OLD TESTAMENT

AND

OUR LORD'S PARABLES.

————

PART I.

PREFACE

THE pictures contained in Part I. of this volume are by some of the most eminent English artists; they will, therefore, serve not only to give a dramatic interest to the more important events recorded in the Old Testament, but also help to cultivate the artistic taste of those into whose hands they may come; while in Part II. twenty pictures, illustrating our Lord's Parables, are given by Sir John Millais, who spread the work over a period of six years, enabling him to give that care and consideration to his subjects which the beauty as well as the importance of the Parables demanded.

CONTENTS—(Part I.).

————◆————

CONTENTS—(PART II.).

CAIN AND ABEL.

The Bible begins by telling us that the world was made by GOD. He created all living things which move upon the earth; and last of all, He made a man and gave him power to know and love Him. The man was to rule over other creatures, and to obey GOD with a joyful and thankful heart.

The first man, Adam, and his wife, Eve, disobeyed GOD; and their sin spoilt the happiness of life on earth, for it brought fear, and pain, and sorrow into the world.

Cain and Abel were the sons of Adam and Eve. Cain helped his father to till the ground and sow corn for food; and Abel took care of sheep.

The young men wished to try and please GOD by offering a sacrifice to Him. They built two altars with heaps of stones. Cain laid some fruit upon one altar, while Abel killed a lamb and placed it upon the other. This was the way in which the men of very early times worshipped GOD. They knew that all things were given to them by GOD; and instead of thanking Him in prayers as we do, they spread their offerings on an altar, under the open sky, hoping that GOD would look down from heaven, and accept the gifts as a sign of their thankfulness to Him.

Abel was a good man, and GOD was pleased with his sacrifice; but Cain was wicked, and GOD would not accept his offering.

Then Cain was very angry; and he grew jealous of Abel and hated him. One day when the brothers were in the fields, Cain rose up against Abel and killed him. As soon as the wicked deed was done, Cain turned away to hide his face, for he could not bear to see his young brother lying, stretched out upon the ground, white and silent in death. In the picture by Sir Frederick Leighton, we see him making haste to fly from the spot, yet choosing a dark path under high rocks, as if he were afraid to show himself in the open country.

NOAH BUILDING THE ARK.

The people that were born into the world, after Adam and his children were all dead, lived very wicked lives. Some of them were giants; and they had no fear of GOD's anger against sin.

The Bible tells us of one good man, called Noah, who taught his sons to obey GOD.

The LORD told Noah that He meant to bring a flood of waters upon the earth, to destroy the wicked people and all living things; but Noah's family and some of every kind of bird, beast, and insect, were to be saved alive.

And GOD told Noah how to build a great ship, which is called an Ark. There was to be a window at the top and a door at the side of the Ark; and it would be like a large house floating on the waters.

Noah began to build this ship at once; according to all that GOD commanded him, so did he. And he gathered together all kinds of food that were eaten.

The wicked people laughed at Noah and tried to tempt him to forsake his work. They used to come with wine, and invite the good man to drink and be merry with them. Mr. Watts has drawn a picture of Noah and his sons, working with bare arms and breasts, under the hot summer sun, while the idle men of the place are watching them, and mocking at Noah's grave face and warning words.

NOAH BUILDING THE ARK.   G. F. WATTS, R.A., DELⁿ.

1.—THE DELUGE.
2.—THE ARK ON THE WATERS.

When the Ark was finished, GOD told Noah to go in with his sons, Shem, Ham, and Japheth, and their wives, and to take two of every kind of living creature, and seven of those used for sacrifices, such as oxen, sheep, and doves.   And the LORD shut them in.

After seven days the rain began to fall, and for forty days and nights it never ceased pouring down from the heavy, black clouds.   The rays of the sun could not pierce the damp air; and in Mr. Dalziel's picture we see the people wandering about in the darkness, seeking for safety upon rocks and hills.   The strength of the giants was of no use to them; they could not escape from their punishment.   Every day the flood rose higher, until at last the land was covered, and no spot of earth was to be seen.   All living creatures were drowned.

In the second picture, the Ark can be seen, floating upon the top of the waters; and everything in it was perfectly safe.   When the rain ceased, and Noah saw clear sky through the window, he let a raven fly out.   It did not come back; it went forth to and fro, until the waters were dried up from off the earth.   After seven days he sent out a dove, but she could find no rest for the sole of her foot, and soon flew home.   After another seven days, he let the little bird fly again; and she returned with an olive leaf in her mouth.   The third time he sent her she did not come back at all; and Noah knew that the land must be nearly dry.

The Ark is a type of Christ's Church.   As Noah and his family were received into the Ark, and kept in safety from the Flood, so by Holy Baptism we are received into Christ's Church, that being washed from sin, and made pure and good by the power of the Holy Spirit, we may pass in safety through the waves of this troublesome world to the land of everlasting life.

4

THE DELUGE.

T. DALZIEL, DEL^{T.}

THE ARK ON THE WATERS.

T. DALZIEL, DEL^{T.}

NOAH'S SACRIFICE.

The Ark had rested upon a high mountain, called Ararat; and GOD told Noah to come out with his family and all living creatures.

As the little company of men and women walked down into the valley, their hearts must have been filled with thankfulness to GOD for having saved them alive, to see the blue sky, and feel the warm sun, and tread the green earth once more.

Noah built an altar; and he burned some of the beasts and fowls upon it, as a sacrifice of praise and thanksgiving to GOD for His great mercy.

The LORD GOD accepted the sacrifice as a sign of His servant's love; and He blessed Noah and his sons. He gave the earth to them, as He had given it to Adam; and He commanded them to spread themselves over the world, that it might be filled with people.

And GOD promised Noah that He would never again send a flood to destroy all living creatures. The rainbow was to be the sign of this promise; it was set in the heavens for a token of the covenant which GOD had made between Himself and all flesh that is upon the earth.

In Mr. Watts' picture Noah is standing in front of the altar, looking up to heaven, and praying GOD to accept his offering. He is holding the knife with which he has killed the birds and beasts; and the smoke of the burning sacrifice is rising into the air. The young men and women, kneeling on the ground, have caught sight of a rainbow in the sky; and they are gazing in fear and wonder at the strange and beautiful sight of the many-coloured bow in the cloudy heavens. Noah's face is turned to the sun, and he has not yet seen the token of GOD's covenant.

NOAH'S SACRIFICE.

G. F. WATTS, R.A., DELᴛ.

1.—ABRAM INSTRUCTING SARAI.
2.—ABRAM PARTING FROM LOT.

Many hundred years after the flood, when the people of the world had forgotten the GOD of Noah, He made Himself known to a man called Abram.

Abram was very rich; he had numbers of sheep and oxen, and men and women-servants. They all lived in tents, and moved from place to place in search of good grass for the cattle.

Abram had a very beautiful wife called Sarai; and when he went down into Egypt with his flocks and herds, he was afraid that the Egyptians would kill him that they might take possession of Sarai; therefore he told Sarai to say she was his sister.

In Mr. Dalziel's picture Abram and Sarai are standing in their tent, talking together. Abram is telling Sarai to call herself his sister. Egypt is a very hot country, and Abram and Sarai are dressed in cool, loose garments, with coverings on their heads to shield them from the sun. The fringed curtain of the tent is lifted with a pole to let in air and light; and we can see a stone-jar for water or milk, and a cup and basin set on the ground near the opening. Inside the tent there are large baskets, and other packages. Two dogs are standing in the shadow cast by the curtain, and beyond them there are cattle in the field, and the tents of Abram's servants.

GOD brought Abram and Sarai safely out of Egypt; and they settled in the Land of Canaan.

Abram's nephew, Lot, travelled about with him, until they became too large a company, and were obliged to separate, because the servants quarrelled.

In the second picture Abram and Lot are standing on the top of a bare and stony hill; and Abram is pointing to the lovely valley of the Jordan, where Lot was to take his family. Lot looks sad as he leans upon his staff; he does not like to leave his uncle and to settle down near strange cities. The shepherds are busy gathering the flocks together and driving them into the plain, where the tents are pitched.

8

ABRAM INSTRUCTING SARAI.

T. DALZIEL, DEL.ᵀ

ABRAM PARTING FROM LOT.

T. DALZIEL, DEL.ᵀ

MELCHISEDEK BLESSES ABRAM.

After Lot had settled in the Plain of Jordan, there was war in the land ; and he was carried away captive by four kings from the north. The news was brought to Abram, who made haste to gather an army together and follow the enemy.

They came upon the kings' camp at night, and after a fierce battle rescued Lot and his family, and all his goods, besides many other people of the land ; and they carried away much spoil from the tents.

As Abram was bringing the prisoners home, he was met by the king of Sodom, and Melchisedek, the priest-king of Salem.

Melchisedek was a holy man, a priest of GOD Most High ; and he blessed Abram and brought out bread and wine, that they might eat and drink together.

In Mr. Solomon's picture we see them all inside a tent. Abram is standing with bowed head and clasped hands before Melchisedek, while a young servant is raising the aged king's arm, that he may lay his hand on Abram's head to bless him. Melchisedek wears a priest's mitre and flowing robes ; his hair and beard are very long, and he is leaning upon a staff. Abram is dressed like a warrior. There is armour under his long cloak and upon his feet, and his hair and beard are short. The king of Sodom stands behind Abram. He has not been to the war, and wears his turban and long cloak as usual. The bread and wine are upon a little table near Melchisedek, and there is a stool standing under the table.

Abram gave Melchisedek a tenth part of the spoil taken from the enemy's camp. This Melchisedek, who was both priest and king, was a type of our Blessed LORD, who is "a Priest for ever after the order of Melchisedek." The BREAD and WINE are types of the Holy Communion.

MELCHISEDEK BLESSES ABRAM.   S. SOLOMON, DEL^{r.}

ABRAM AND THE ANGEL.

When Abram returned to his camp at Mamre, the word of the LORD came unto him in a vision. He had already told Abram that He would give the Land of Canaan to his family, and that they would become a great nation, in whom all other families of the earth would be blessed; and now He bade Abram look up at the stars in heaven, for his children should be as numerous as the stars.

Abram had not one child yet; it was a great trouble to him, and it was very hard to believe that his family would grow into a great nation. But the angel told him that he would surely have a son, and that the Land of Canaan would belong to his race.

In Sir Frederick Leighton's picture of the vision, the angel is standing by Abram's side, pointing to the countless stars shining in the clear heavens. There is a halo of glory round his head, and he has a holy and beautiful face, which is turned towards Abram, as he comforts him with the promise of a son. They are in the open air, and the moon is shining brightly. We can see the hedge, which was placed round the camp to keep wild animals from getting near the tents, and over the hedge there is the outline of a hill in the distance. Abram is looking up at the stars, wondering at the promise which has just been made to him.

ABRAM AND THE ANGEL.   SIR F. LEIGHTON, P.R.A., DEL^{T.}

ABRAHAM AND THE THREE ANGELS.

When many years passed, and no child was born to Sarai, Abram took another wife called Hagar, who had a little son; and Abram thought that this boy, Ishmael, was the child promised to him by the LORD. But it was not so. The LORD told Abram that Sarai would be the mother of a son, and as a sign of the promise, she was to be called "Sarah," which means "Princess," or "Mother of Kings," and Abram's name was to be changed to "Abraham," or "Father of a Multitude."

One very hot afternoon, Abraham was sitting just inside the tent door, when he saw three strangers walking towards him. He got up directly, and asked them to come into the shade, and wash their feet, and rest, and have some food before going on their way. The men agreed to do so, and sat down under the trees.

Then Abraham told Sarah to bake some cakes of fine meal for his guests, and he ordered a young calf to be cooked for them.

After the meal, one of the men, who were messengers from GOD, told Abraham that Sarah would have a son during the next year. Sarah, who was standing close to them, behind the curtain of the tent, laughed when she heard this old promise; but the man reproved her by saying that nothing was too hard for the LORD.

In the picture by Mr. Solomon, Abraham is inviting the three strangers to rest in his tent. He has risen hastily and come out with bare feet to meet them, and he is holding the hand of one, as if persuading him to accept the invitation. The angels are noble-looking men, dressed in flowing robes like princes, not as if they were accustomed to work. They carry staves, but they do not look tired from their walk. The tents are pitched near a grove of trees, which gave shelter from the burning mid-day sun.

ABRAHAM AND THE THREE ANGELS. S. SOLOMON, DEL.^{T.}

1.—THE DESTRUCTION OF SODOM.
2.—ABRAHAM LOOKING TOWARDS SODOM.

The three angels went on their way towards Sodom, one of the cities of the Plain of Jordan; and as Abraham walked with them, he heard that Sodom was to be destroyed because of the sins of the people. They lived very wicked lives, doing exactly what they wished, without thinking if it were right or wrong. Had there been ten righteous men in the city, the LORD would have spared it, but Lot and his family only were to be saved alive.

Two of the angels went to tell Lot to take his wife and daughters out of Sodom. They must leave at once, before morning, and hurry on to the mountains, without stopping for one moment to look back towards the city.

In Mr. Dalziel's first picture, we see Lot with his two daughters, one on each side, hurrying on to the mountains for safety. Behind them, Lot's wife is standing still, looking back towards Sodom. The mist of early morning lies upon the hills, but the valley is lighted up by the vivid glare of the burning city. The woman was punished for her disobedience to the angel's command. As she stood upon the brow of the hill, to take a last glance at her old home, she became like a pillar of salt.

Early next morning Abraham left his tent to look out towards Sodom; and in the second picture we see him standing on the road, watching the clouds of thick smoke rising up out of the valley.

THE DESTRUCTION OF SODOM.   T. DALZIEL, DEL^T.

ABRAHAM LOOKING TOWARDS SODOM.   T. DALZIEL, DEL^T.

HAGAR AND ISHMAEL.

Not long afterwards Sarah had a little son, and Abraham called him Isaac.

Ishmael was thirteen years old, and until this new baby came, he had been treated as his father's heir. It made him angry to know that Isaac would be the head of the family, and he was unkind to his little brother.

GOD told Abraham to send Hagar and Ishmael away, because the children would certainly quarrel if they lived together in their father's tent.

In Mr. Solomon's picture, Abraham is standing just within the tent, looking sadly after Hagar and his eldest son, as they set out on their journey to seek a new home. Hagar looks very unhappy, and her arm is round the boy, as if she would draw him closer to herself, because he would no longer have a father to watch over him. Ishmael is stepping forward eagerly. He has a bow in his hand, and he knows how to shoot birds with arrows; perhaps he is thinking with pleasure of the long walk across the country, where he can shoot what he likes. We can see that the tent is pitched amongst trees, and there are two wild pigeons lying upon the ground, while one is flying about the tent.

GOD watched over Hagar and Ishmael, and Ishmael became the father of the Arab tribes.

HAGAR AND ISHMAEL.   S. SOLOMON, DEL^T.

ABRAHAM AND ISAAC.

Isaac grew up a good and obedient boy; and his father loved him dearly.

Abraham never forgot the promises of GOD; and he had faith to believe that they would all be fulfilled. Isaac would be the father of a great nation who would dwell in the Land of Canaan.

GOD would try His servant once more, to see if he would obey any command, however hard. He said to Abraham: "Take now thy son, thine only son, whom thou lovest, even Isaac, and offer him for a burnt-offering upon one of the mountains that I will tell thee of."

It was the very hardest command that could have been given to Abraham. He was to give back to GOD a life, that was dearer to him than his own. Yet he did not hesitate to obey GOD; and early next morning he set out to go to the mountains.

Isaac went with his father; and in the picture drawn by Mr. Solomon, the old man and his young son are walking in the open country below the mountains. It is spring-time; they are treading upon wild flowers; and there are a number of storks flying in the air, seeking food for their young ones. Isaac has been gathering wood for the sacrifice, and he is asking his father, where was the lamb for the burnt-offering? Abraham has laid one hand upon the boy's head, and with the other he is lifting Isaac's right hand to kiss it. He could not bear to tell the child that he is to be sacrificed himself; and he answered: "My son, GOD will provide the lamb" Abraham looks very sad; his heart is torn with sorrow at the thought of parting with his bright and beautiful young son. Isaac's linen tunic is quite loose round the throat, and his head is protected by a covering something like a fisherman's helmet.

ABRAHAM AND ISAAC.   S. SOLOMON, DEL^T.

ABRAHAM'S SACRIFICE.

Abraham and Isaac went up the mountain; and Abraham built an altar and laid the wood in order, and bound Isaac, his son, and laid him upon the altar; and he stretched out his hand and took the knife to slay his son. Just as he was going to strike, the voice of an angel called to him out of heaven, "Abraham, Abraham, lay not thine hand upon the lad, neither do anything to him, for now I know that thou fearest GOD, seeing that thou hast not withheld thy son, thine only son, from Me."

In Mr. Solomon's picture an angel with outstretched wings has caught Abraham by the wrist; and the old man is looking up into his face, as if he were startled by the voice and, touch. Abraham's other arm is round poor Isaac, who looks dreadfully pale and frightened. A ram is caught by its horns in a bush hard by; and when Abraham has set Isaac free, he will offer it up as a burnt-offering instead of his son.

Afterwards GOD renewed His promises to Abraham; and He said, that through his family all other nations would be blessed.

The mother of our Lord Jesus Christ was of the family of Abraham; and when He was born in Bethlehem this promise was fulfilled.

The sacrifice of Isaac is a type of the death of our Lord Jesus Christ, who offered Himself a perfect sacrifice to God, in obedience to God's will; and having passed through death, He rose again (even as in a parable Abraham received Isaac back from the dead). It is also a type of the Holy Communion, in which we show His death until His coming again. By the power of His Spirit, He gives all men strength, by faith to offer themselves, body, soul and spirit, to the Father, even as Abraham offered Isaac.

ABRAHAM'S SACRIFICE.   S. SOLOMON, DEL^{T.}

ELIEZER AND REBEKAH.

When Isaac was grown up into a young man, Abraham sent his servant, Eliezer, to fetch a wife for his son from Haran, where his father's family lived.

Eliezer loaded ten camels with all sorts of beautiful things for presents to his old master's relations; and he set out to cross the desert in search of a wife for Isaac.

When he reached the city, he made the camels kneel down near the well outside the gates; he did not know where Nahor, Abraham's brother, lived, and must ask the way.

It was the cool evening-hour, just before dark, when the women of the city came out to draw water for their households; and in Sir Frederick Leighton's picture, Eliezer is watching them come down the steps to go to the well outside the gates. The first woman is tall and beautiful; and she is holding a stone water-jar very gracefully upon her shoulder. She wears earrings and a large necklace, and there are bracelets upon the upper part of her bare arm, and on her wrist. Her under-garment is of some soft, white stuff, over which she is holding a long, dark cloak. The woman has a proud air, and looks as if she were of higher rank than those who are following her. There are some shrubs with broad leaves growing near the steps. and Eliezer is standing in their shadow.

He did not know that the beautiful maiden was Nahor's daughter.

ELIEZER AND REBEKAH.   SIR FREDK. LEIGHTON, P.R.A., DELᵀ.

ELIEZER AND REBEKAH AT THE WELL.

Eliezer believed that the GOD of Abraham ruled over the world and all the people in it ; and he prayed to Him, that He would let it come to pass, that the woman whom Isaac was to marry, should be the one who would give him water to drink.

When Rebekah had drawn some water from the well, Eliezer went up to her, to ask for a drink.

The maiden made haste to let the pitcher down from her shoulder again, and gave it to Eliezer ; and afterwards she drew some water for the camels.

Then Eliezer asked her name, and when Rebekah said that she was the grand-daughter of Nahor, he knew that GOD had answered his prayer ; and he told Rebekah that he had come from Abraham.

In Mr. Holman Hunt's picture, we see Eliezer and Rebekah standing together at the well, outside the city of Haran. Eliezer has unpacked some of the presents, carried by the camels. He has given Rebekah two brace-lets of gold, and is putting large earrings into her ears. Eliezer hoped that this lovely young maiden would consent to go back with him ; and the presents showed that Isaac was the son of a rich man. We can see the strong walls of Haran on the top of the hill ; and the well is covered with hewn stone. There is a large hole for the water to run through, so that the women may not have any trouble in drawing it. There are not many trees in the fields ; and the ground looks sandy and barren. The camel which had just been unloaded is near at hand, but we cannot see the others.

ELIEZER AND REBEKAH AT THE WELL.   HOLMAN HUNT, DEL.ᵀ.

1.—ISAAC MEETING REBEKAH.
2.—ESAU SELLING HIS BIRTHRIGHT.

Nahor was dead; and Eliezer went to the house of Laban, the brother of Rebekah, and stayed there.

Rebekah was quite willing to be Isaac's wife; and in a few days Eliezer started for home again. He took Rebekah and her old nurse, and some of her women-servants, back with him.

In Mr. Dalziel's picture, we see the company of camels and drivers standing on the road in the light of the setting sun. Eliezer has told Rebekah that Isaac is coming towards them; and she has got down from her camel to wait for him. She is holding a veil over the lower part of her face, after the manner of women in eastern countries, but her eyes are fixed upon Isaac, who is hastening to meet his bride.

Isaac and Rebekah had two sons, Esau and Jacob. Esau was fond of hunting, but Jacob liked a quiet life. Esau, being the eldest son, would be the head of the family when Isaac was dead. It would be his duty to offer the sacrifices, and rule over the others.

In the second picture, Esau and Jacob are sitting together in one of the tents. Esau has just come in from hunting, and is quite faint from hunger and weariness. He has thrown himself down on a low seat, and his spear is resting against the cushion. One of his dogs is already fast asleep, and the other is going to lie down. Esau wears a short tunic made of fur, and his arms and legs are quite bare. Jacob is sitting upon a stool near the opening of the tent. He has made himself soup, and was going to drink it, but Esau has asked for some.

Jacob said that Esau might have the soup, if he would give up the rights of the eldest son; and Esau promised that Jacob should be head of the family, instead of himself.

Rebekah is standing in the background behind Esau, and she has heard all that passed. Through the tent-door, we can see a camel drinking at a trough and a servant near it; and there are more tents in the distance.

ISAAC MEETING REBEKAH.   T. DALZIEL, DEL^T.

ESAU SELLING HIS BIRTHRIGHT.   T. DALZIEL, DEL^T.

ISAAC BLESSING JACOB.

When Isaac was an old man, he became blind and very feeble; and he wished to bless his eldest son, before he died. He told Esau to shoot some game and cook it for him; and he promised to give him his last blessing, when he had eaten it.

Rebekah loved Jacob best; and she wished her favourite son to have the blessing.

While Esau was away hunting the game, she cooked some savoury meat for Isaac, and gave it to Jacob to carry in to his father.

Isaac could not see his sons, but he liked to pass his hand over their faces; and because Esau was a hairy man, Rebekah covered Jacob's hands and neck with the skin of kids, so that his father might not notice their smoothness; and she brought some fine raiment belonging to Esau, and put it upon her youngest son.

In the picture by Mr. Armytage, Isaac is giving Jacob that last blessing which ought to have been kept for Esau. The old man has taken Jacob's hand; it feels hairy; and he knows the touch and smell of Esau's raiment. He believes that he is blessing his eldest son. There is a spear and shield on the wall above Isaac's couch; and a low table with a water-jar upon it stands at his side. Jacob is dressed in Esau's beautiful raiment. It has some fur about the neck, and a border round the bottom; and it is fastened with a broad coloured sash. Rebekah is standing with the dish in her hand, listening to Isaac's words. She is pleased that her favourite son should have the birthright and the blessing, which belonged by right to Esau.

ISAAC BLESSING JACOB.

E. ARMYTAGE, R.A., DEL.

JACOB MEETING RACHEL.

Esau was very angry with Jacob for robbing him of his father's last blessing; and he said that he would kill his brother.

Rebekah sent Jacob to his uncle, Laban, at Haran, that he might be out of Esau's way; and she hoped he would find a wife amongst his cousins.

Laban had two daughters, Leah and Rachel. Rachel was very beautiful; and Jacob loved her dearly. He agreed to be Laban's servant for seven years, if he might have Rachel for his wife; but at the end of the seven years, Laban gave Leah to Jacob instead of Rachel. Jacob was very angry because he could not force Laban to keep his promise.

In those days men often had two wives; and Jacob offered to serve Laban for another seven years, if he might have Rachel at once, as a second wife. Laban agreed to the bargain; he was glad to secure a clever and faithful servant.

Mr. Dyce has drawn a picture of Jacob and Rachel in the fields together. We can see how dearly the young man loved his beautiful cousin. Love is shining on his face; and he is holding her hand to his heart. Rachel has come out of the city to draw water from the well; and her jar is standing on the stone-covering. Jacob has left his uncle's sheep lying in the sunshine, to come and speak to Rachel. He wears a shepherd's tunic made of sheepskin; and a stone-jar for water is slung at his side. Rachel's cool linen garment is bound round her waist with a coloured sash; and she has a dark covering on her head. Jacob is bending forward to kiss her.

JACOB MEETING RACHEL.　　　　　　　W. DYCE, R.A., DELᵀ.

1.—JACOB AND THE FLOCKS OF LABAN.
2.—JACOB'S DEPARTURE FROM LABAN.

At the end of fourteen years, Jacob wished to go back to Canaan; but Laban persuaded him to stay at Haran and serve him for wages. It was settled that all the black sheep, and all the goats with speckled and spotted skins, should belong to Jacob, no matter how many were found in the flocks at spring-time.

In the picture drawn by Mr. Dalziel, the sheep and goats have been driven down to the water to drink. They have long horns like rams, and look strong and healthy. There are four young shepherds with Jacob, who wear sheepskin tunics and have water-jars slung at their side; but Jacob is a master now, and he has a loose linen robe with a coloured border, and sandals upon his feet. He is carrying a bundle of rods, which are to be placed at the edge of the stream amongst the reeds. The water is quite shallow; and the sheep can go down and stand amongst the stones to drink. The country is very pretty on this side of Haran; and there are a good many trees.

Laban was vexed because a great many lambs fell to his nephew's share of the flocks; and he was quite ready to quarrel with Jacob over them.

It was not the will of GOD that Jacob should stay at Haran; and He told him to take his family and all his flocks to Canaan.

In the second picture, we see the great company starting on their journey. They are travelling by night, and are in haste to get out of the country, before Laban can overtake them. Jacob is walking first, and his two wives, Leah and Rachel, are close behind him. One of his young sons has taken his right hand, and he is holding a staff in the left. A youth, who has the charge of two dogs, tied together with a cord, is walking in front of the camels. We can see their ugly heads in the moonlight, and the figures of the drivers, perched on the top of great bundles of goods.

It was pleasant to walk in the moonlight, but when the sun rose and it became hot, the women and children would be lifted on to the backs of the camels.

34

JACOB AND THE FLOCKS OF LABAN.   T. DALZIEL, DELᵀ·

JACOB'S DEPARTURE FROM LABAN.   T. DALZIEL, DELᵀ·

ESAU MEETING JACOB.

When Jacob reached the Land of Canaan, he heard that Esau was coming to meet him with four hundred armed men. He was dreadfully frightened, and he prayed to God to take care of him and his wives and children.

That same night the Lord appeared to Jacob and told him that he was no longer to be called Jacob, but Israel, which means a "Prince of God"; and Jacob knew that God had heard his prayer.

Mr. Watts has drawn a picture of the meeting between Esau and Jacob. At the first sight of his only brother all the anger died out of Esau's heart, and instead of trying to kill Jacob, he has laid his hands upon his shoulders and is bending forward to kiss him. Esau is a tall, fine-looking man, dressed in a short hunting tunic, and a case full of arrows is fastened to his coloured belt. His head is uncovered, as if the short, thick hair were enough protection from the sun; he has rough, strong sandals upon his feet. Jacob wears a long, loose cloak with a hood to throw over his head. He is much surprised at Esau's warm greeting, and can hardly believe that his brother has forgiven him.

Esau had an open and generous nature, and Jacob was deceitful; yet we must not forget that it was Jacob who prayed to God and believed in His promises, while Esau cared for nothing but hunting.

From this time the family of Jacob are generally called " Children of Israel," or Israelites, after the new name which God had given to Jacob.

ESAU MEETING JACOB.   G. F. WATTS, R.A., DELT.

JOSEPH'S COAT.

Jacob had twelve sons. Joseph and Benjamin, the two youngest, were his favourites, because they were the children of his beloved Rachel. The elder brothers were jealous of Joseph. He was a very clever boy, and he dreamed strange dreams, which seemed to mean that he would be the head of the family. Jacob gave Joseph a beautiful coat to wear instead of the rough shepherd's tunic, and kept him at home, when the other brothers were taking care of sheep on the hills.

Once, Jacob sent Joseph into the country to bring him news of his brothers' welfare; and the men stripped the boy of his beautiful coat, and threw him into an empty pit. Afterwards they sold him to some merchants who were going to Egypt; and upon returning home, they said they had found the coat covered with blood.

In the picture by Mr. Madox Brown, Jacob is sitting upon a high seat in his tent, and little Benjamin is close to him. Two men are showing Joseph's coat, which is torn in one place and has marks of blood upon it. It is a white linen tunic with a broad, richly-coloured border, and it has long loose sleeves and some embroidery at the throat. A dog, in a collar with bells, is smelling at the spots of blood, and a young woman is pointing to them. They are all looking at poor old Jacob, and saying that some wild beast must have killed his dearly beloved son. Jacob is tearing his clothes in an agony of grief, and little Benjamin has left off playing on his lute to listen to the men. One man is carrying his sandals, and the other holding out the coat.

JOSEPH'S COAT.   F. MADOX BROWN, DEL^{T.}

JOSEPH BEFORE PHARAOH.

Joseph was sold for a slave to an officer of Pharaoh, king of Egypt; and after serving his master faithfully for several years, he was unjustly accused of wrong-doing and thrown into prison.

Joseph was a good man, and the LORD was with him in prison. It became known that he could understand the meaning of dreams; and when king Pharaoh had two strange dreams, he sent for the Hebrew slave to come and explain them to him.

In Mr. Poynter's picture we see Joseph standing before Pharaoh in a beautiful marble hall. The king has just told him that he dreamed of seven lean cows eating up seven fat cows, and of seven thin ears of corn eating up seven full ears. Pharaoh's face is very grave and stern; he has fixed his eyes upon Joseph, while his hands are clasped tightly upon his knees. His dark hair is bound with a circlet of gold, and there are heavy golden bracelets upon his wrists. He wears a robe with a beautiful border of needlework. Joseph is standing before him in a slave's dress; but he looks like a young prince. He is a noble-looking youth with a handsome face and fine figure; and as he raises his finger and throws back his head, looking straight into the king's face, Pharaoh must see that this Hebrew was not born a slave. A man of humble birth would not have stood upright with one foot on the step, and he would not have dared to tell Pharaoh the meaning of his dreams. Joseph is saying that, after seven years of great plenty in Egypt, there will be seven years of famine; and he warns Pharaoh to prepare for the famine. The queen, on the couch at the other end of the room, is smiling at the warning, and one of the officers has raised his hand in scorn. A little slave is playing with a tame stork, and another is holding a fan behind the king's chair.

JOSEPH BEFORE PHARAOH.　　　　　E. J. POYNTER, R.A., DEL^T.

PHARAOH HONOURS JOSEPH.

Pharaoh saw that the spirit of GOD was in Joseph; and when the young Hebrew told the king, that the corn of the seven years of plenty ought to be saved up for the seven years of famine, he said that Joseph himself should rule over the land, and prepare for the famine. If GOD had shown him the meaning of the dreams, then His spirit would also teach him how to save the people from hunger.

In Mr. Poynter's second picture, the scene is laid in another marble hall of the palace. Pharaoh has risen from his throne to put a ring on Joseph's right hand; and there is a golden chain lying on the little table which he will place upon the new minister's neck, as a sign that he is a ruler of the land. The king's royal mantle of tiger-skin is thrown over a white linen robe with a coloured border, and he wears a circlet of gold with an ornament in front. The queen remains seated upon the throne, and is looking earnestly at the young Hebrew. Joseph is clothed in pure white linen; one hand is upon his heart, and he has bent his head before Pharoah. The officers of the court stand behind Joseph; and there is a row of slaves. holding fans made of peacocks' feathers, on one side of the throne In the background a man is playing softly upon the harp.

Joseph knows that it is the LORD GOD of Abraham who has taken him out of prison to be a ruler over the Land of Egypt; and he has no fear of the king, nor of the officers who may be jealous of his power.

PHARAOH HONOURS JOSEPH.

E. J. POYNTER, R.A., DELT.

JOSEPH DISTRIBUTES CORN.

For seven years there was abundance of corn in Egypt, and Joseph went through the land to buy up all that was not needed for food. The merchants were not allowed to take any out of the country; it was all stored in dry barns in the cities.

At the end of the seven years a famine came upon the land, and there was no corn. Then Joseph opened the barns and began to sell what he had stored.

In the picture by Mr. Poynter, Joseph is sitting at a table in an office. He is talking to a woman, who has just bought some corn and is carrying it away in a flat basket upon her head. Two little children are with her, both of them quite naked; but she does not look poor; her white dress is embroidered with colours, and she wears earrings and bracelets, and a heavy necklace. A man, with a bottle of ink hanging at his side, is keeping an account of the money paid to Joseph; and another clerk, standing near the door, is writing on a tablet. All the women are carrying flat baskets or jars for the corn. Through the open door, we can see men taking sacks of corn out of the barn, to be weighed in the yard. Joseph has a small pair of scales in front of him, that he may weigh the rough coins to find out their full value. There are two sacks, full of money, upon the floor near him, and a beautiful casket for small bags, which probably contain gold or silver coins, is placed near them.

JOSEPH DISTRIBUTES CORN.

E. J. POYNTER, R.A., DEL^T.

JACOB HEARS THE VOICE OF GOD.

During the famine, Joseph's ten elder brothers came to Egypt to buy corn. They did not know him again, but he recognised them directly, and asked many questions about their family.

He longed to see his young brother Benjamin, and he kept Simeon in Egypt, until the others brought Benjamin to him. Then he made himself known to them as Joseph, whom they had sold for a slave. The brothers were afraid that he would punish them, but instead of that, he treated them all very kindly, and sent them back to Canaan to fetch his old father, Jacob, to come and live in Egypt.

Jacob could hardly believe that his beloved Joseph was still alive, and he said, "I will go and see him before I die." He offered sacrifices to the God of Abraham, and prepared to leave Canaan at once with all his family.

In a vision of the night the LORD spake unto Jacob, saying, "Fear not to go down unto Egypt—I will there make of thee a great nation, and I will surely bring thee up again to Canaan."

Mr. Sandys has drawn a picture of the vision. It is night, and we can see the cattle lying on the ground in the dim light of the crescent moon. Jacob has been asleep on a mat in his tent, and he has put his left hand on the pillow to try and raise himself. With the right hand he is shielding his eyes from the brilliant light of the Heavenly Vision. He has been awaked suddenly by the Voice of GOD.

JACOB HEARS THE VOICE OF THE LORD.   F. SANDYS, DEL^T.

JOSEPH PRESENTS HIS FATHER TO PHARAOH

Joseph was very much beloved by Pharaoh and the Egyptians, and they were glad that he should have the happiness of seeing his old father again.

In the picture drawn by Mr. Poynter, Joseph is presenting Jacob to the king. Pharaoh is leaning back on a beautiful couch in an open court-yard, paved with coloured marbles. He is not wearing the tiger-skin, and there are no officers in the court. This is a friendly visit. Pharaoh wants to talk quietly with the father of his favourite. Joseph has thrown a cloak with a coloured border over his white linen robe, but his left hand is free to help his old father. Jacob looks very feeble, and is leaning heavily upon Joseph's shoulder, and upon his shepherd's staff. He wears a long coloured cloak with a striped border and a fringe, and his white hair is covered with a turban. There are women and slaves in the court who look curiously at the figure of the old Hebrew, as his son leads him proudly and tenderly before the king. Pharaoh spoke very kindly to Jacob, and they talked together for some time.

There are trees planted in large pots round the court, and the sunshine is streaming on the marble floor and pillars, throwing up the strange coloured figures of men and animals.

48

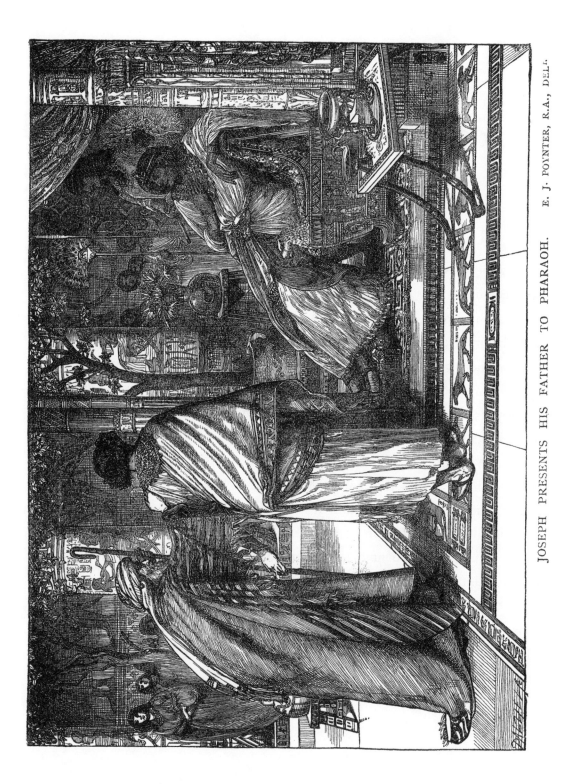

JOSEPH PRESENTS HIS FATHER TO PHARAOH.   E. J. POYNTER, R.A., DEL.

JACOB BLESSING EPHRAIM AND MANASSEH.

Jacob and his family settled in the open country, in a place called the "Land of Goshen," and Jacob lived for many years in peace near his beloved son.

Joseph married an Egyptian lady, and had two sons, Manasseh and Ephraim; and when Jacob grew very old, he took these boys to receive their grandfather's last blessing. Joseph cared more for his place in the family of Abraham, than for all the riches and honour to be won in Egypt; and he was very anxious that Ephraim and Manasseh should not miss their share in the promises of GOD.

In the picture by Mr. Pickersgill, Jacob is sitting up on a low couch with his arms round the boys. Manasseh is looking up into his grand-father's face, as if he loved him dearly, but Ephraim has dropped his head to hide his tears. Joseph is kneeling in front of Jacob, holding his sons by the hand; he has bent his head and is looking very sad. Old Jacob's face is calm and peaceful; he knows that death is near, but he is not afraid, and he is very thankful to have the great happiness of knowing Joseph's sons and giving them his last blessing. He said that Ephraim and Manasseh would be the fathers of two great tribes, who would have a share of the Land of Canaan.

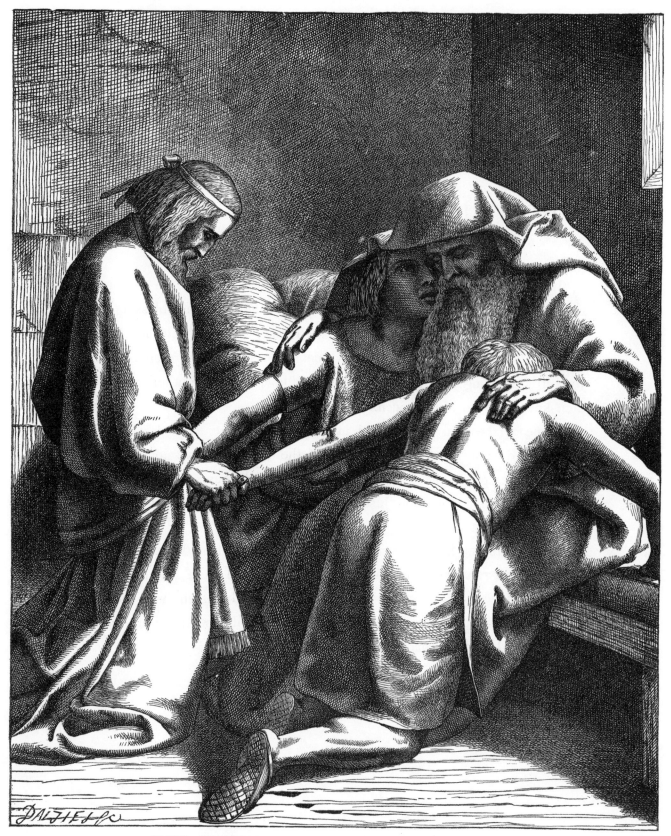

JACOB BLESSING EPHRAIM AND MANASSEH.   F. R. PICKERSGILL, R.A., DEL.ᵀ

JACOB BLESSING HIS TWELVE SONS.

In Mr. Dalziel's picture Jacob is lying upon a couch in his tent, surrounded by his twelve sons. He is giving them his last blessing and foretelling the future of their families. Although very old and feeble, he has strength to raise his hands and speak to each of the men by turn. Joseph is kneeling on a stool close to the pillow, and three others are upon their knees in front of the couch.

Some of the men are dressed in long loose garments, tied round the middle, and some wear cloaks. All of the brothers have long beards excepting Joseph. The Egyptians always shaved themselves, and being an officer of King Pharaoh, Joseph shaved his face and wore pure white linen robes.

Jacob is telling his sons that the tribe of Judah will hold the first rank, when they all return to Canaan, and that Joseph will have a double share of the land because his two sons, Ephraim and Manasseh, will each be head of a great tribe; and he foretold that the tribe of Benjamin would mingle with Judah and share Judah's blessings.

T. DALZIEL, DEL^r.

JACOB BLESSING HIS TWELVE SONS.

THE INFANT MOSES.

After many years the family of Jacob grew into a great tribe, which filled the "Land of Goshen"; and the Egyptians began to fear that these Israelites would become more powerful than themselves. They treated them as slaves, and at last a king arose who determined to destroy them altogether. He commanded that every boy, born in an Israelite family, should be thrown into the river Nile.

Most of the Israelites had forgotten the GOD of Abraham and all His promises to their race, and they worshipped the gods of Egypt. At last GOD raised up a prophet from amongst them to teach them about Him, and to lead them out of Egypt back into the Land of Canaan. His name was Moses, and he was saved out of the river Nile by Pharaoh's daughter and brought up as her son.

In Mr. Solomon's picture we see Moses as a big baby in his mother's arms; she has kept him hidden for three months in the house. He is a beautiful boy, strong and healthy; and she is holding one of his little fat hands and looking into his face. His sister Miriam, who helped to hide the boy, has a basket under her arm. They are going to put Moses into the basket, and place it amongst the rushes on the banks of the river. It was possible that some Egyptian lady might take pity on the lovely baby, and save it from being drowned.

When the princess came to bathe in the river she found Moses and determined to save him. Miriam, who was near at hand, offered to get a nurse for the baby, and she fetched her own mother; but Moses was brought up as the son of Pharaoh's daughter.

THE INFANT MOSES.   S. SOLOMON, DELᵀ.

MOSES SLAYING THE EGYPTIAN.

Moses was very clever, and he learned everything that the wise men of Egypt could teach him; but he never forgot that he was an Israelite, and he took pains to find out all about his own people. He longed to help them. His heart burned with anger when he saw them cruelly used by their masters.

One day he came upon an Egyptian beating a Hebrew slave; and it made him so angry that he killed the man.

In Mr. Poynter's picture, Moses is standing over the Egyptian with one hand pressed upon his throat, so that he cannot cry out, and the other grasping a mallet. He is looking down the road to see if anyone is near; and he does not notice a man's head peering over the unfinished wall. His beard shows that he is an Israelite by birth, but there is a heavy golden collar on his throat and a circlet of gold round his head. He has thrown off his long cloak, and the short striped skirt leaves him quite free to struggle with the man. The whip, which the Egyptian has used to flog the slave, is leaning against the wall, and the Israelite has escaped. The flat red bricks are made of the mud of the Nile, mixed with straw, and baked in the sun, and we can see how they are fitted in together without mortar.

The Egyptians are building a temple, or a hall of some kind, and all the heavy work is being done by Israelites under taskmasters. Beyond the table in the shade, there are slaves busy at work upon the walls.

MOSES SLAYING THE EGYPTIAN.   E. J. POYNTER, R.A., DELᵀ.

MOSES KEEPING JETHRO'S SHEEP.

King Pharaoh heard that Moses had slain an Egyptian, and he sent to find him ; but Moses had already fled into the Land of Midian.

It was a wild country, with high rugged mountains and deep valleys. The people were shepherds, who wandered about with their flocks and herds in search of wells and green grass.

Moses found shelter with Jethro, a priest and chief of the land. He married one of Jethro's daughters and lived the life of a shepherd.

It was a great change from Egypt and King Pharaoh's court; and Moses had time to think of the sorrows of his own race and of the wonderful promises of the GOD of Abraham.

At the end of many years GOD spoke to Moses, and told him that he must go back to Egypt and lead his people into the Land of Canaan. He promised to be with Moses, and to make King Pharaoh afraid of keeping the Israelites in the land.

Mr. Poynter has drawn a picture of Moses taking care of his sheep in the wilderness. Moses has a clever and most sympathetic face; he looks as if he were thinking of the poor Israelite slaves in Egypt, and wondering if the GOD of Abraham would really come to their help; and, although lost in sad thoughts, he has stretched out his hand to one of the sheep, who is licking it. His tender heart overflows with love; and there is enough to spare for the dumb animals. Moses wears a loose coloured garment, in which he can wrap himself when night comes on. The country is rocky and barren, but there is enough coarse grass for these hardy mountain sheep.

MOSES KEEPING JETHRO'S SHEEP.   E. J. POYNTER, R.A., DELT.

MOSES AND AARON BEFORE PHARAOH.

————

Moses had an elder brother named Aaron, and God spoke to him also and sent him to meet Moses. The two brothers went first into the Land of Goshen, and called together the elders of Israel to tell them that the God of their fathers had promised to save His people out of the hands of King Pharaoh, and to bring them to the Land of Canaan.

The Lord God had given Moses power to work miracles with the shepherd's staff before Pharaoh, and before the Israelites, as a sign that he and his brother were sent by God.

In Mr. Poynter's picture we see Moses and Aaron in one of Pharaoh's marble halls. The king is sitting upon a throne, raised on several steps and covered with a canopy. Behind him a number of slaves are standing in the sunshine, waving fans of peacocks' feathers to keep the air cool. Moses is on the top of the steps, close to the throne; he has told the king that they have been sent by the God of Israel, to ask that His people might go for three days into the wilderness, to offer sacrifices to Him. Pharaoh is refusing to listen to Moses. He has raised his left hand as a sign to him to go away; but Moses is not in the least afraid of Pharaoh, and only comes nearer to repeat the words in a more threatening voice.

Aaron is standing below the steps. He has thrown the rod of Moses on to the ground, and it has changed into a serpent. The Egyptians have put an ugly image of a god on the pavement with two little vessels full of burning incense in front of it; and they have also thrown down their small rods. The rods changed into serpents, but Aaron's serpent is running after them to swallow them. The wise men are looking at Aaron in wonder, and some of them have bent their heads before him.

When Aaron picked up the serpent it changed into a shepherd's staff again; but Pharaoh's heart was hardened and he would not believe in the power of the God of Israel.

60

MOSES AND AARON BEFORE PHARAOH.　　E. J. POYNTER, R.A., DELT.

1.—THE WATER TURNED INTO BLOOD.
2.—THE BOILS AND BLAINS.

Then GOD sent plagues upon the land of Egypt.

Moses lifted up his rod and smote the River Nile; and the waters of the river became red as blood. All the fish died, and there was a dreadful smell in the land.

In Mr. Dalziel's first picture we see the poor people on the banks of the river, trying to find water. Some of them are digging in the sand, hoping that a little will rise up, and one woman is holding out a saucer to beg for a few drops. The water-jars are lying about empty; and the women and children are dying from thirst. The deep, calm river is glistening in the sunlight; but neither the storks nor the cattle can drink of its waters. For seven days they were like blood.

GOD sent plagues of frogs, and lice, and flies upon the land; and all the cattle died of a grievous sickness.

Yet Pharaoh still refused to let the Children of Israel go to offer sacrifices; and he would not listen to Moses and Aaron.

Then GOD told Moses to sprinkle handfuls of ashes in the air, and the small dust would bring boils upon man and beast.

In Mr. Dalziel's second picture we see Moses and Aaron in the distance, on the other side of the river. They have met Pharaoh and his courtiers in front of the palace, and Moses has just scattered the ashes into the air. The small dust is coming in a cloud, across the water towards the people sitting on the pavement, at the edge of the river on the opposite bank. Some of them have already been taken ill; four are sitting down and seem to be in great pain, while the man in front is looking at them in astonishment. The dust has not yet reached the two women with a dog, who are sitting upon a low table, eating a meal.

62

THE WATER TURNED INTO BLOOD.   T. DALZIEL, DEL^T.

THE BOILS AND BLAINS.   T. DALZIEL, DEL^T.

THE ISRAELITES IN EGYPT. WATER-CARRIERS.

In Mr. Poynter's picture of the water-carriers, we see two Israelite women with heavy stone jars upon their heads. The bottom of each jar is bound round with a cloth to make it easier to carry. They are very handsome women, with large, dark eyes and long hair; one has a bracelet on the upper part of her bare arm, and the other wears a chain.

They are going down to the Nile for water. We can see the river gleaming in the distance, and the dim figures of two women standing on the stone wall above it with jars upon their heads, while another woman is stooping down to fill hers.

The wall, in the foreground of the picture, is covered with strange figures, which are painted upon the bricks.

E. J. POYNTER, R A., DEL.

THE ISRAELITES IN EGYPT.—WATER-CARRIERS.

THE PASSOVER.

GOD sent a dreadful thunderstorm, and a plague of locusts; and afterwards it was perfectly dark in Egypt for three days; yet still King Pharaoh refused to obey His voice.

Then GOD told Moses that the Israelites were to keep a Feast, called the "Feast of the Passover." The father of each household was to kill a lamb and roast it with fire; and it was to be eaten with unleavened bread (that is, bread made without yeast) and bitter herbs. The people were to eat it in haste, dressed ready for a journey, with staves in their hands. The lamb was to be killed before twilight, and the father was to sprinkle the two side-posts and the upper door-post of his house with blood; for in that same night the LORD GOD would pass through the land of Egypt and smite all the first-born of the land, and when He should see the blood on the door-post, He would pass over that house and would not enter in to destroy the first-born.

In the picture we see the father of an Israelite family in the act of sprinkling his door-post with blood. He has killed the lamb, which is lying on a stool just outside the door; his eldest son is holding a basin, full of its blood, while the sister has herbs in her hand. There is the mother with a baby in her arms; and a young child is clinging to her skirts. They have all tied up their garments to be ready for a journey, but they have not yet put on their sandals. The lamb has to be roasted and eaten in the evening.

The lamb of the Passover is a type of Christ; it was to be perfect, without blemish, and no bone was to be broken. The blood of the lamb was sprinkled on the door-posts, as a sign that the Angel of Death must pass over that door, and not enter in to destroy the first-born. The blood of our LORD Jesus Christ was poured out upon the cross, when He offered Himself a perfect sacrifice to GOD; and we make a memorial of that sacrifice to the Father in the Holy Communion, and pray the Father for Christ's sake to save us from sin and spiritual death, and to send His Holy Spirit into our hearts to help us to turn from evil ways, and do His will as Christ did.

66

THE PASSOVER. S. SOLOMON, DELᵀ.

DEATH OF THE FIRST-BORN.

At midnight, while the Israelites were eating the Feast of the Passover, the LORD smote all the first-born in the land of Egypt, from the eldest son of Pharaoh to the first-born of the humblest slave in the dungeon. A great cry arose in the land, for there was not a house where there was not one child lying dead. The Israelites heard the cry and knew what had happened; the hour of their deliverance was at hand.

In Sir Frederick Leighton's picture we see a young man in great pain; he has pressed one hand to his side, and with the other he is clutching the woman who is nursing him. An old physician is standing on the far side of the bed with a sponge in his hand. He has dipped it into the basin, held by a negro slave, and is going to bathe the sick man's face. The mother is kneeling at the foot of the bed, with her clasped hands uplifted to heaven in an agony of grief; and there is another woman in the background with her hands up to her face. Through an opening in the wall, we can see the dark figure of an angel with a drawn sword in his hand. It is night, but the room is lighted up.

Below the large picture are three smaller ones. In one, the foal of an ass is lying dead, and in another the son of a woman in prison. They are both fastened to the wall, and the mother cannot get to her son. In the middle one Pharaoh himself is bending over his first-born son; and at last he confesses the power of the GOD of Israel.

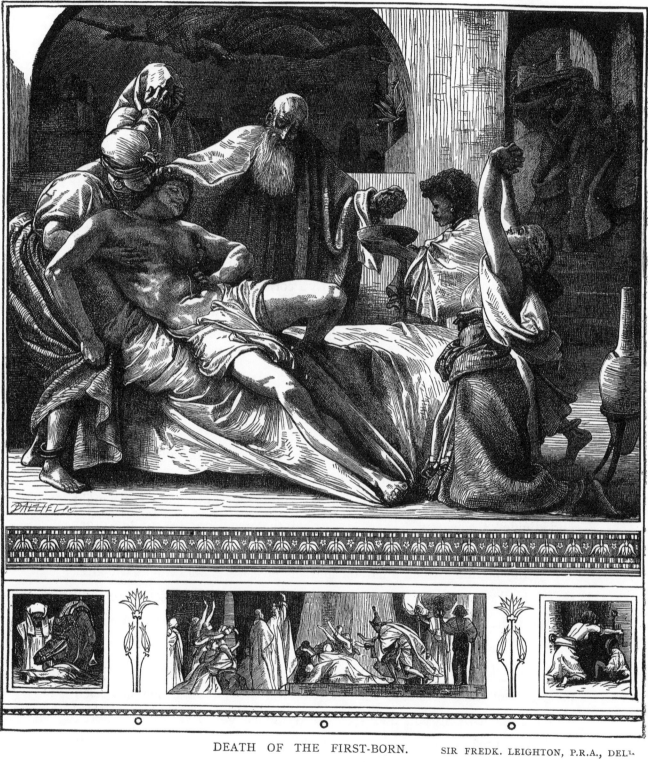

DEATH OF THE FIRST-BORN.   SIR FREDK. LEIGHTON, P.R.A., DEL.

1.—DEPARTURE OF THE ISRAELITES.
2.—DESTRUCTION OF PHARAOH
AND HIS HOST.

Pharaoh rose up in the night, and, calling in haste for Moses and Aaron, he commanded them to go away out of the country at once, with all the Israelites and their flocks and herds. Moses had already made plans for the journey to the Land of Canaan, and the people were quite ready to start that same night.

In Mr. Dalziel's first picture we see them marching along, carrying their children and bundles of all sorts and sizes. One boy has a torch; and there are some dogs running about. In a corner of the picture an Egyptian woman is weeping over her first-born son. The sun is rising behind the city and throwing a low light over the figures; but the sky is still dark, and a few stars can be seen.

In a very short time Pharaoh repented that he had let the Israelites go, and he gathered together a great army to follow after his slaves and bring them back again. The Israelites had reached the shores of the Red Sea, and GOD told Moses to stretch his rod out over the waters, and there would be a dry path in their midst.

Moses obeyed the command, and a strong east wind blew all the night and divided the waters. Then Moses led the people across to the other side in safety.

In the morning, when Pharaoh and his host were following hard after them, the LORD told Moses to stretch out his rod over the sea again, and in a moment the waters began to roll back and cover the path. Pharaoh and all his host were drowned in the sea.

In Mr. Dalziel's second picture we see Pharaoh and his warriors, and their chariots and horses, in the midst of the waters. The sun has risen over the Land of Egypt, and they are trying to get back to the shore; but it was useless to struggle against the rushing waves, and not one of them was saved.

DEPARTURE OF THE ISRAELITES.　　　T. DALZIEL, DEL^r.

DESTRUCTION OF PHARAOH AND HIS HOST.　　　T. DALZIEL, DEL^r.

MIRIAM.

The LORD had saved Israel out of the hands of Pharaoh and his host; and they saw the Egyptians dead upon the sea shore. Then Moses and the children of Israel sang before the LORD; and Miriam, the sister of Moses and Aaron, took a timbrel in her hand, and all the women went out after her with timbrels and with dances.

In Mr. Poynter's picture, we see the women singing songs of praise and thanksgiving, and dancing before the LORD. Miriam is tall and very beautiful; her dark hair is bound with a circlet of gold, and partly covered with a white veil, which floats behind her. She wears a heavy jewelled necklace, and beautiful bracelets on her arms and wrists. Her robe is quite loose, allowing her to move gracefully in a slow dance, as she sings and shakes her timbrel. The women and the children are all dressed in embroidered garments, and they are all dancing and singing to the music of the timbrels. Moses and the men are higher up on the hill, overlooking the sea; and we can see a waggon drawn by two oxen, and some sheep driven by a shepherd.

Some of the jewels and beautiful robes, worn by the Israelite women, were given to them by their Egyptian neighbours, on the night they left Egypt. In their fear of the GOD of Israel, the Egyptians had given their slaves whatever they asked for, and the Israelite women had begged for jewels and fine raiment.

The Red Sea is a type of Holy Baptism. As the Israelites passed through the sea on their way to the Promised Land, so we, through Baptism, enter into the rest and peace and safety of Christ's Church. Canaan was to be the home of the Chosen Race, and the Church of our LORD is the home of His faithful people, where they are ruled by His laws, and protected and strengthened by His Holy Spirit.

MIRIAM.

E. J. POYNTER, R.A., DEL^T.

GATHERING OF MANNA.

The Children of Israel marched from the shores of the Dead Sea through the wilderness, and whenever they came upon wells or springs of water, the tents were pitched, and they took a longer rest than usual. A pillar of cloud went before them by day and a pillar of fire by night; and wheresoever it led, they were obliged to follow.

When the supply of bread failed, the people began to murmur against Moses; and they said, he had brought them into the wilderness to die of hunger.

GOD told Moses that He would feed the people; in the morning they should have bread.

When the sun had risen, and dried up the dew that lay about the camp, a quantity of small round seeds, like hoar-frost, covered the ground. Moses told the people that this was the bread sent to them by GOD, and it would lie upon the ground every morning. They must rise early and gather sufficient for one day, before the sun was hot enough to melt it.

In the picture by Mr. Houghton, we see the people gathering the manna. Three little children have got some in their skirts, and are showing it to two old men with long beards. All the men wear cloaks as a protection from the chilly morning air, but some of the very young children are nearly naked. The women are busy gathering the manna and putting it into pots like water-jars.

They took it to their tents, and after grinding it in a mortar, baked flat cakes; and the taste was like wafers made with honey.

Manna is a type of Christ. Jesus Himself said that He was the bread, which came down from Heaven. The Israelites needed manna for daily food, to keep them strong and well in the wilderness; and in like manner our souls are fed and strengthened by Christ. Everyone who asks for help to do what is right, will feel the power of Christ's Holy Spirit, strengthening his soul; and in the Sacrament of the Lord's Supper we spiritually eat the flesh of Christ, and are made strong by it.

GATHERING OF MANNA.   A. B. HOUGHTON, DEL^T.

MOSES' HANDS HELD UP.

When the Israelites pitched their tents in the Valley of Rephidim, they were attacked by another tribe of shepherds, who wanted the water and grass for their own flocks and herds.

Joshua, a young warrior, full of faith and courage, led the people to meet these Amalekites in battle; and Moses went up to the top of a hill, in the middle of the valley, to cry to GOD for help. He could be seen from all sides, standing with the rod in his hands, praying to the LORD for victory. Aaron and Hur, the husband of Miriam, were with him; and all day long the three men stood together, watching the battle below. When Moses held up his hands in prayer, the army of Israel was victorious, and when they dropped down from weariness, the warriors of Amalek drove the Israelites back.

At last Moses grew so tired that Aaron and Hur made him sit down upon a stone, and they stayed up his hands, one on each side, until the sun went down.

In Mr. Pickersgill's picture of the three men, Moses is looking up to heaven, praying earnestly to GOD for his people; Hur has turned his head to watch the battle in the valley, and Aaron's eyes are fixed upon his brother's face. The hill is stony and barren, but there are wells and a stream bordered by palm-trees in the valley; it is one of the few green places in the Wilderness of Sinai.

GOD heard the prayer of His servant Moses, and, in the evening, Joshua drove the Amalekites out of the valley.

MOSES' HANDS HELD UP. F. R. PICKERSGILL, R.A., DELT.

MOSES DESTROYS THE TABLES.

Three months after the Israelites left Egypt, the tents were pitched on a great plain below the cliffs of Sinai.

The LORD GOD came down upon Mount Sinai in fire and smoke, and the people heard the voice of a great trumpet exceeding loud; and the LORD called Moses to come to the top of the Mount. Moses went up into the cloud upon the top of Sinai, and stayed there forty days and forty nights. GOD told him what to do for the Israelites; and He gave him two tables of stone with the ten commandments written upon them.

Meanwhile, the Israelites were tired of waiting for their leader, and they had not yet learnt that the GOD of Moses was the only GOD. They asked Aaron to make them a golden calf, such as they had seen in Egypt; and they said that this god, which was made out of their own golden earrings, should go before them into Canaan.

In the picture by Mr. Armytage, we see Moses and his servant Joshua coming down the cliffs. They are standing above the plain, where the round tents are pitched, and they can see the golden calf and the people all round it. A great feast is going on, and the noise of singing and dancing reach their ears. Moses has the tables of stone in his hand, and in his wrath he is just going to dash them down against the rock, when they will be broken into pieces.

His anger waxed hot against the people; and the ringleaders were slain with the sword.

Afterwards, Moses prayed the LORD to forgive them their great sin; and the LORD heard the prayer of His servant. He commanded Moses to hew two tables of stone like unto the first; and He wrote upon the tables the words that were on the first tables.

MOSES DESTROYS THE TABLES.   E. ARMYTAGE, R.A., DELT.

THE PEOPLE PRESENTING GIFTS
TO MOSES.

The LORD GOD told Moses to make a beautiful Tabernacle, or "Sacred Tent," for the Israelites. It was to be set up in the middle of a court, and the court was to be enclosed by curtains, hung from pillars of brass. The sacrifices were to be offered upon a great altar in this court; and there was to be a golden altar for incense inside the Tabernacle.

It was the will of GOD, that this Tabernacle, and all the beautiful things inside it, should be made of the gifts of the people. Therefore, Moses told the Israelites to bring, of their own free will, whatever they wished to give.

In Mr. Pickersgill's picture, we see Moses standing before an open chest, receiving the free-will offerings of the people. One woman is taking earrings from her ears to give to the man kneeling in front of the chest, and another woman is telling her little child to put in a bracelet. There is some cloth lying upon the ground, and a third woman is bringing more; it is to be used for the curtains of the tent; and fine white linen will be wanted for the robes of the priests. We can see ornaments, and a cup and basin of brass, lying on the top of the chest, which is quite full now. Moses is leaning upon his staff, looking down at the things, and Aaron is behind him.

In the distance, some men are carrying wood to make boards for the sides of the Tabernacle, over which a roof of curtains is to be thrown.

THE PEOPLE PRESENTING GIFTS TO MOSES.   F. R. PICKERSGILL, R.A., DELT:

MOSES CONSECRATING AARON.

The tribe of Levi were to take charge of the Tabernacle, and Aaron, who was the prince of the tribe, was to be the first High Priest. The men of his family were to be the priests, and to offer sacrifices upon the great altar in the court.

Mr. E. Armytage has drawn a picture of Moses, consecrating Aaron to be High Priest of the LORD. Aaron has knelt down before his brother; and Moses is placing a mitre of pure white linen upon his head. Aaron's right hand rests upon the breastplate, which was made of a square piece of fine linen, embroidered with blue, purple, scarlet and gold; and upon it were fastened twelve precious stones, each one of a different kind, engraved with the names of the twelve tribes of Israel. It was kept in its place by blue cords, running through small golden rings, which were stitched on to the edge of the square, and on to the robe, or ephod, as it was called. This ephod was also made of linen, embroidered with colours. The long cloak was of blue woollen stuff, and little bells of gold, and pomegranates made of coloured wool, were stitched all round the bottom of it. The man behind Moses is holding a golden crown, to be fastened upon the mitre with a blue cord; the words, " Holy to the LORD," are engraved upon it. Moses and Aaron, and his sons, have washed their hands and feet; and the ewer of water is still standing on the laver. One of the elders of Israel has charge of the ox for the first sacrifice upon the great altar; and we can see the heads of a crowd of people in the court, waiting for Moses and Aaron to come out.

Christ is our High Priest. He offered Himself for us; and now he stands at the right hand of GOD to make intercession for us, as Aaron did for the Israelites; and to plead in Heaven, as His priests and people do on earth, His sacrifice on the Cross, that we may be able to follow His example. The bishops, priests, and deacons of the Christian Church are, like the priests and Levites of old, set aside by GOD for the service of His sanctuary.

MOSES CONSECRATING AARON.

E. ARMYTAGE, R.A, DELᵀ.

THE FIRST OFFERING OF AARON.

In this picture, Aaron has come out into the court, and is going to offer a sacrifice. He has taken off the mitre, and robe, and breastplate, and is raising his hands in prayer to GOD before slaying the victim. Two young priests, in linen ephods and mitres, are standing near their father, and one is holding the ox by the cord. It is a fine animal, decorated with garlands of flowers. The elder, who brought it to be sacrificed, is going to lay his hands upon it, as a sign that it is his gift; and the young man, on the other side, is holding the cord firmly in both hands. The priest beyond him is carrying a brazen vessel of incense; and another young priest has a lamb in his arms. We can see the curtains hanging round the court, and beyond are the trees of the plain where the tents are pitched.

THE FIRST OFFERING OF AARON.

S. SOLOMON, DEL^T.

THE BURNT OFFERING.

When the people brought a burnt offering, or free-will offering, the whole animal was burnt up on the altar. They were a sign that the offerer gave himself up to GOD, and was ready to do His will in all things.

In the picture, Aaron is standing in the court near the great altar. He has killed the ram with the knife, lying upon the little table, and has poured some of its blood into a basin; and now he is holding the victim towards heaven, before placing it upon the fire, burning on the top of the altar. Afterwards he will sprinkle the altar with its blood. Aaron is dressed in the blue robe with its fringe of bells and pomegranates. In the light of the fire, we can see the offerer and two priests, kneeling in front of the altar, and behind them are three figures, near the curtains of the court. The priests wear white linen mitres, and the other men have large turbans twisted round their heads. It is evening, and the sun is low in the heavens.

A burnt offering is a type of Christ, because He offered Himself willingly to GOD, and gave His body to be crucified that His sacrifice might be perfect and entire, even as the burnt offering was wholly consumed by the fire. Christ gave Himself up, body, soul and spirit, to do the Father's will; and in fighting against sin, He suffered and was buried; but He rose again from the dead, and by the power of His Spirit helps us in our warfare against wickedness in ourselves and in the world.

THE BURNT OFFERING.   S. SOLOMON, DEL^{T.}

OFFERING INCENSE.

Incense was made of fragrant spices, mixed with frankincense, and beaten into a powder; it was burnt upon the golden altar, inside the Tabernacle, every morning and evening, while the Israelites prayed in the court outside. They knew when the High Priest entered the Holy Place to burn the incense, by the tinkling of the golden bells upon his robe.

In the picture, Aaron is standing in the Holy Place of the Tabernacle, preparing the incense for the morning sacrifice. One priest is holding the censer, while Aaron with a golden spoon is taking more spice out of a vessel, held by another. A little curl of smoke is already rising from the censer; and it will soon fill the place with a fragrant odour. One of the young priests is playing upon a musical instrument, and another has a spray of some herb in his hand. The wooden walls of the building are overlaid with gold, and there is a beautiful curtain at one end to separate the " Holy Place " from the " Holy of Holies."

Inside the " Holy of Holies " there was a chest, overlaid with gold, in which the tables of stone were kept; this chest was called the Ark; and afterwards other sacred relics were put into it.

OFFERING INCENSE.   S. SOLOMON, DEL^{T.}

OFFERING THE FIRST-FRUITS OF THE HARVEST.

The Israelites offered all first-fruits to GOD; they did not begin their harvest until a sheaf ot new corn had been brought to the altar.

In the picture we see the High Priest, standing in the court of the Tabernacle, waiting to receive the first-fruits. Two men are carrying large baskets, filled with pomegranates, upon their shoulders; and there is a basket of grapes upon the ground. One of the young priests is carrying a censer, and another is playing upon a musical instrument. It is summer, and the sun is very hot; most of the men wear turbans and loose linen garments. A flock of sea-birds are flying across the sky to the shores of the Dead Sea.

S. SOLOMON, DELᵗ

OFFERING THE FIRST-FRUITS OF THE HARVEST.

"HE SHALL ORDER THE LAMPS."

The Holy Place was lighted by a golden candlestick with six branches. At the end of each branch was a lamp full of olive oil, which was kept burning day and night.

In this picture, we see Aaron and his sons filling the small lamps with oil. These lamps and all the vessels were made of pure gold; and it was one of the duties of the priests to clean them and keep them in order. A youth is pouring oil into the lamp which Aaron holds, and another is placing those that are ready upon the candlestick; he lights one from another, as he puts them up. The other sons are looking on, and the youngest of all is leaning against his elder brother. All the priests wear their white linen ephods and are barefooted. They leave their sandals outside the Tabernacle. The candlestick is very large and handsome; it is nearly as tall as Aaron.

"HE SHALL ORDER THE LAMPS."   S. SOLOMON, DEL^T.

THE SPIES BRINGING THE GRAPES.

When the Israelites reached the borders of Canaan, Moses sent twelve men of the princes of the tribes to spy out the land, and he told them to bring back some of the fruit to show the Israelites.

In Mr. Pinwell's picture we see the spies, returning to the camp with beautiful fruits. One cluster of grapes is slung upon a staff and carried by two men, and the others are following with figs and pomegranates. The young man walking first is Joshua; his face is glowing with happiness as he tells the people of the rich cornfields, and vineyards, and olive-groves of Canaan; he is a prince of the tribe of Ephraim. The elder man, who bears the other end of the staff upon his shoulder, is Caleb, a prince of Judah. These two bring a good report of the land; and Caleb said to Moses, "Let us go up at once and possess it."

But the other spies began to speak of the people of the land; some of them were giants and very strong, and they lived in walled cities. These words made the people afraid to go on to Canaan; and they wept all night long, murmuring against Moses and Aaron for having brought them up out of Egypt.

Then the LORD GOD was very angry with the people; and He said that not one of them, excepting Caleb and Joshua, should enter the Land of Canaan.

They were to wander about in the Wilderness of Sinai for forty years, until all the men who were more than twenty years old when they left Egypt, were dead; and their children should possess the land.

94

THE SPIES BRINGING THE GRAPES.   G. J. PINWELL, R.W.S., DELᵀ.

THE REBELS SWALLOWED UP.

———

Soon after the Israelites turned back to wander in the wilderness, a rebellion broke out in the camp, headed by Korah, a Levite, and Dathan and Abiram, princes of the tribe of Reuben, the eldest son of Jacob.

Korah said, Moses and Aaron took too much upon themselves in offering the sacrifices; and Dathan and Abiram murmured because they ruled over the people.

Moses told Korah and the other rebels to come to the Tabernacle next morning, that they might burn the incense for the early sacrifice; and the LORD GOD would surely make it known, if it were His will that all the Levites or only the family of Aaron should be priests.

Two hundred and fifty of them came with censers; and Moses warned the congregation to keep away from the Tabernacle, and not to go near the tents of Korah, Dathan and Abiram, for GOD would surely punish the rebellion. He had scarcely finished speaking when the ground clave asunder, and the earth opened her mouth and swallowed up the tents of the rebels, and their households, and all their goods; and the earth closed upon them, and they were seen no more.

In the picture by Mr. Pickersgill, Moses is standing with uplifted hand, looking down upon the men as they disappear into the earth. We can see two of them, clinging to stones to save themselves from going down. A man is holding two women fast by the arm, as if to drag them away; one has fallen on her face, but the other is holding up a baby. If they are of the family of the three rebels, they will be destroyed by the earthquake; for GOD will show His people once for all, that it is His will that Moses should be their leader, and any rebellion against him will meet with punishment.

THE REBELS SWALLOWED UP.   F. R. PICKERSGILL, R.A., DELT.

THE DEATHS OF KORAH AND THE LEVITES.

Meanwhile, Korah and the two hundred and fifty Levites who had joined him, were burning incense for the morning sacrifice. The fire on the altar and in the censers did not rise up before GOD; it spread about on all sides and caught their robes; and all the Levites who carried censers were destroyed by the flames.

In the picture we see Moses and Aaron in the Holy place of the Tabernacle, looking with horror at two of the men who have fallen backwards, struck by the scorching blast from the altar. The flame is following them to burn them as they lie there on the ground; a censer is slung by a cord upon the arm of one man; his eyes are open and he seems quite conscious; the other looks as if he were already dead. Moses has been speaking words of warning to the Levites, and his finger is still uplifted, while Aaron, who is clothed in his high-priestly robes, has been watching them in silence, waiting for the punishment sure to come upon the rebels. The golden vessels, which the Levites have dared to use, are standing on the table near them.

THE DEATHS OF KORAH AND THE LEVITES.   E. ARMYTAGE, R.A., DEL^T.

MOSES STRIKES THE ROCK.

At the end of forty years the Israelites came to Kadesh, near the borders of Canaan. The tents were pitched on a plain below the steep, red cliffs of Edom, and murmurs arose in the camp because there was no water to drink.

God told Moses to gather the people together, and to take his rod and speak to the rock before their eyes that it give forth water.

Moses took his rod and called the Israelites to come after him to the cliffs; but, instead of speaking to the rock as God commanded, he cried, "Hear now, ye rebels, shall we bring you forth water out of this rock?" And Moses lifted up his hand and smote the rock with his rod twice, and water came forth abundantly.

In Mr. Poynter's picture a stream of water is rushing down from the top of the cliffs, and the thirsty people are filling jars of all shapes and sizes. One man, who has no jar, is stooping down to drink from the stream, and another is giving some to his little child. Every one of the crowd is either drinking or filling a jar, or holding water for someone else to drink. Moses is standing on higher ground than the people, with the rod in his hand; and Aaron, who is near his brother, has just filled a water-jar from the stream and is handing it to a woman. The mountains are very high and barren, and there are no sheep upon them.

MOSES STRIKES THE ROCK.   E J. POYNTER, R.A. DELT.

THE DEATH OF AARON.

The LORD GOD was grieved with Moses because he had disobeyed
His voice. He had cried, "Must we fetch you water, ye rebels?" as if
he could bring forth water from the rock by his own power. Therefore
GOD said that Moses and Aaron were not to pass over the river Jordan
and lead the people into Canaan. Moses might see the land from afar,
but Aaron must go to the top of Mount Hor and die there.

Aaron put on his high-priestly robes for the last time; and he
climbed up Mount Hor with Moses and Eleazar, his eldest son, in sight
of all the people.

Mr. Armytage has drawn a picture of the three men on the top
of the Mount. Aaron is lying on a rough couch, covered with sheepskin,
and there is an awning over his head to protect him from the sun.
His eyes are closed, and one arm is hanging over the side of the couch;
he looks very old and at the point of death. Moses has taken off his
brother's high-priestly robes and is putting them upon Eleazar. The
young man is kneeling with clasped hands before his old uncle, waiting
to have the blue robe thrown over him; and the mitre is lying upon
the ground close at hand. Moses is looking up to heaven. It must be
a hard trial for him to lose his brother; but he has faith in GOD and
bears his trouble meekly, as part of the punishment for disobeying GOD.

When Aaron was dead, Moses and Eleazar came down the Mount
alone; and Eleazar was clothed in the high-priestly robes.

THE DEATH OF AARON.　　　　　E. ARMYTAGE, R.A., DELT.

THE BRAZEN SERPENT.

After the death of Aaron the Israelites marched on through the wilderness towards Canaan; and the soul of the people was much discouraged because of the rough way. There was not enough water for the great multitude, and they were tired of manna; therefore they murmured against GOD and against Moses, saying, "Why have ye brought us up out of Egypt to die in the wilderness?"

And the LORD sent fiery serpents amongst them, and they bit the people and many died of their wounds.

Then Moses prayed the LORD to forgive their great sin, and He heard the prayer of His servant.

GOD told Moses to make a serpent of brass and to set it upon a standard; and He said that, if anyone who was bitten looked up to the serpent, he should be healed.

In the picture by Mr. Pickersgill the brazen serpent is hanging upon a cross, and the hand of Moses rests upon the beam. A young mother is holding up her baby that it may look at the serpent and live; and a man is raising a girl in his arms that her face may be turned towards it. The Israelite, lying upon the ground, is trying to throw away the serpent twined about his neck; if he turns round and looks up, he also will be healed. Moses is very sad; his eyes are fixed upon the young mother, but he is lost in thought; perhaps he is wondering what will become of these rebellious Israelites when he is no longer there to cry to GOD to forgive them.

The Brazen Serpent is a type of Christ. Jesus was lifted up upon the Cross that we might look at Him and be healed of the wounds made by sin. Trusting in the love which moved Him to offer the sacrifice for us, we plead in the Holy Communion the same sacrifice, and cry for help in our weakness, and His Spirit pours new life into our sick souls.

THE BRAZEN SERPENT.   F. R. PICKERSGILL, R.A DELT.

BALAAM AND HIS ASS.

On the way to Canaan the Israelites conquered the Amorites and took possession of their strongholds; and Balak, the king of Moab, was afraid that his cities (and pasturelands) would fall into their hands; therefore, he sent for the Prophet Balaam to come and curse the Israelites.

GOD told Balaam that he must not go to Moab with the messengers, for He had blessed Israel.

Then the king sent again, promising to promote Balaam to great honour, if he would come and curse the Israelites; and this time GOD spoke to Balaam, saying, "Rise up and go with the men; but only the word which I speak unto thee that shalt thou do."

Balaam saddled his ass and went with the princes of Moab; but his heart was not right with GOD; he wished to win silver and gold, and great honour from Balak; and he could not please the king without disobeying GOD. The anger of the LORD was kindled againt the Prophet, and He sent an angel to meet him. The ass saw the angel and stumbled in trying to get out of his way. Three times Balaam smote the ass; and then he heard her speaking to him, asking, why he had smitten her?

Balaam looked up, and seeing the angel standing in the way, he understood why the ass had stumbled.

In the picture by Mr. Waltges, Balaam has got down from his ass to throw himself upon his knees before the angel. The figure of the angel almost fills up the narrow road between the vineyards, and the ass is standing quite close to the wall on one side. The angel has a sword in his hand; he has come to warn Balaam that his perverse thoughts are known to GOD. Balaam is saying that he will turn back and go home, but the angel answers that he must go on, and speak whatever word GOD puts into his mouth.

Therefore, instead of cursing Israel as Balak wished, Balaam prophesied that the people would be blessed above other nations.

BALAAM AND HIS ASS.   F. S. WALTGES, DELT.

THE DAUGHTERS OF ZELOPHEHAD.

When Moses knew that his end was near, he gathered the people together to tell them how the Land of Canaan was to be divided amongst the tribes of Israel. "His eye was not dim, nor his natural force abated"; and, old as he was, none of them would dare to disobey him.

The daughters of Zelophehad, a man of the tribe of Manasseh, came to Moses to ask if they might not have a share of the "Promised Land"? Their father had never had a son, and these five women were all that were left of his family.

GOD told Moses that the daughters were to have the portion of land that would have fallen to their father; and from henceforth, if a man had no son, his daughters were to inherit the land belonging to him.

Moses said that the women must marry men of their own family, so that the land might not pass into the possession of another tribe; and the five sisters agreed to choose husbands of their father's family.

In the picture by Mr. Pickersgill, the women have come before Moses and Eleazar, and the two men are considering what ought to be done. The eldest daughter has knelt down before them to plead their cause; another who is near her, is quite young, almost a child; the three others are older; they are listening to the conversation between Moses and Eleazar. All the women are beautiful, and they are dressed alike, in loose gowns with short sleeves, fastened by girdles round the waist; and their hair is unbound and very long.

THE DAUGHTERS OF ZELOPHEHAD.   F. R. PICKERSGILL, R.A., DEL^T.

MOSES VIEWS THE PROMISED LAND.

God had promised that Moses should see the Promised Land before he died; and when the great leader had spoken his last words of warning and of blessing to the people, he went up from the plains of Moab to the top of Pisgah.

Sir Frederick Leighton has drawn a picture of Moses, looking at the beautiful country which he might not enter. Canaan lay spread out before him, with its green hills and valleys, and its woods and cornfields; at his feet the river Jordan ran like a silver thread through the deep green valley into the Dead Sea; in the distance there was a dim blue line of the waters of the Mediterranean Sea, in the far north the Mountains of Hermon with their snowy peaks, on the south the yellow desert. It was a wonderful country, and Moses was able to see it clearly, for his eyes were not dim with age. He stood alone there, alone with God and his own memories of the long life which was nearly over.

Moses died on the top of Pisgah, and the Lord God buried him in a valley, and no man knew the place of his sepulchre.

Moses was the greatest of the prophets, and his greatness lay in his unselfish love for his own people. "The Lord knew him face to face." The Israelites might have good and brave captains in the years to come, but never another Moses, the Deliverer and Leader, and Father of his race.

MOSES VIEWS THE PROMISED LAND.   SIR F. LEIGHTON, P.R.A., DEL^T.

"MERCY AND TRUTH ARE MET TOGETHER; RIGHTEOUSNESS AND PEACE HAVE KISSED EACH OTHER."—PSALM lxxxv., 10.

———

Mr. Solomon's picture is an allegory of Righteousness and Peace. The two women are holding each other in a close embrace, and one is kissing the other. There are doves flying about, and these gentle birds are emblems of love. One has alighted upon the shoulder of Peace with a twig of olive in her mouth. The lilies are in full bloom, and the sun is streaming down upon them. It is a lovely scene, full of peace and joy, and the beautiful women are in harmony with nature in her happiest mood.

The allegory is meant to describe the close bond between righteousness and peace. If a man does what is right, if he loves GOD and his neighbour, he is at peace with man and at peace with GOD. The spirit of love dwells in his heart; he looks up to GOD in faith, sure that his Father in Heaven will take care of him; and he is kind and loving and merciful to all men. Because he loves righteousness, his heart is full of peace.

Moses had tried to make his people understand that they could not be happy, nor at peace, unless they did what was right and kept the laws of their GOD; and he warned them of the troubles and punishments that would surely come upon them, if they did evil in the sight of the LORD.

S. SOLOMON, DELᵀ.

"RIGHTEOUSNESS AND PEACE HAVE KISSED EACH OTHER."

RAHAB AND THE SPIES.

Moses had told the Israelites that the LORD GOD had chosen Joshua to be their leader; they must follow him across the Jordan and take possession of the Land of Canaan.

And GOD spoke to Joshua, saying, "As I was with Moses, so I will be with thee, I will not fail thee nor forsake thee. Be strong and of a good courage."

The people were encamped on the banks of the Jordan; and on the other side of the river the City of Jericho could be seen, rising up above groves of palm trees. The Israelites could not get into the country beyond the river without first taking Jericho, and Joshua sent two men as spies to the city; he wanted to know if the Canaanites would bring an army into the plain or shut themselves up behind their high walls.

The men swam across the Jordan and came to the city; and after walking about the streets for some time, they entered into the house of a woman called Rahab to lodge there.

In the picture by Mr. Pickersgill the two men are going quickly upstairs, and the woman is bolting the door. Rahab knows the men are Israelites by their dress and speech, and she does not want any one else to come in. She is a beautiful woman with large eyes and long flowing hair. Her dress is not quite like the garments worn by the women of Israel; it is cut low, and the sleeves are short, and she wears a kind of apron twisted round the skirt. The men have put off their sandals and their cloaks; one is lying on the ground near a large water-jar. They bend their heads while passing the open window as if afraid of being seen. The house was built upon the city walls, and there are gardens and fields below the window where people might be walking.

RAHAB AND THE SPIES.   F. R. PICKERSGILL, R.A., DEL^T

THE SPIES ESCAPE.

——

Not long after the spies came to the house of Rahab the woman was startled by the sound of loud knocking at her door. The men had been seen in the streets, and the King of Jericho had sent to Rahab to bring them out.

Rahab took the two Israelites up on to the flat roof, and hid them under some flax which was drying there. Then she hurried down to the messengers and told them that the men had left her when it grew dark, at the time of the shutting of the city gates. The King's servants did not stop to hear more; they made haste to follow after the spies.

Meanwhile Rahab went up to the roof and told the spies that she had heard of the GOD of Israel, how He had dried up the Dead Sea when the Israelites came out of Egypt, and how He had delivered the mighty Kings of the Amorites into their hands. "The LORD, your GOD, He is GOD in Heaven above and on the earth beneath," said Rahab.

And, knowing that the City of Jericho would surely fall before Joshua and his warriors, she begged the spies to save her life and the lives of her family. The men agreed willingly; and then Rahab let them down by a strong red cord through the window.

In Sir Frederick Leighton's picture one man is swinging himself down from the balcony by the cord; and the other is sitting on the stone balustrade, looking out over the country to see if there is any one about in the fields. Rahab is on the watch at the other side; she has put out her hand as if to warn the men against making any noise; the King's servants are still searching for them.

The men told Rahab to bind the red cord round her window that the Israelites might know her house.

THE SPIES ESCAPE.　　　SIR FREDK. LEIGHTON, P.R.A., DELᵀ.

THE PASSAGE OF THE JORDAN.

The LORD GOD told Joshua that He would work wonders in the sight of all Israel, that the people might know He was with their leader. They had escaped from Egypt by a dry path in the midst of the sea; and He would lead them across the Jordan in the same wonderful way.

The camp was broken up, and the people marched forwards to pass over the river. The priests who carried the ark went first, and as soon as their feet were dipped in the brink of the Jordan, the waters ceased flowing to the Dead Sea, and the bed became dry. The priests that bare the ark stood firm on dry ground in the midst of the Jordan, and all Israel passed over on dry ground. And when the priests that bare the ark were come up out of the midst of the river, the waters returned unto their place.

In Mr. Pickersgill's picture, a group of people on the high banks of the Jordan are watching the priests carrying the ark across the dry bed of the river. The ark is covered with a cloth, and the priests are carrying it by poles, which are passed through rings at the sides. The waters are gathered together in a heap, and we can see the bare stony ground of the river-bed. There is an old blind man sitting in front of the river, and his daughter is telling him what has happened. One woman, frightened by the miracle, is clinging to her sister, who looks out over her head to see the wonderful sight. A man in the background is shading his eyes from the glare of the sun that he may see more clearly. Very soon they will all go down the bank and pass over the dry bed on to the other side of the river.

THE PASSAGE OF THE JORDAN.   F. R. PICKERSGILL, R.A., DEL^T

CAPTAIN OF THE LORD'S HOST—THE ANGEL APPEARING TO JOSHUA.

The Children of Israel pitched their tents near Jericho; and they began to eat of the corn of the Land of Canaan; and from that day they had no more manna.

The people of the city were shut up within their walls; none went out and none came in; and Joshua thought it must be taken by storm.

One night, while walking near Jericho, he saw a man standing over against him with a sword drawn in his hand. Joshua went up to the man and asked him, "Art thou for us or for our enemies?"

And the man answered, "Nay; but as Captain of the host of the LORD am I now come."

Joshua fell upon his face and worshipped him.

And the Captain told Joshua to take his shoes from off his feet, for the place whereon he stood was holy; and Joshua did so.

Then the Captain of the LORD's host told Joshua that the LORD would give Jericho into his hands; the walls should fall down at His command; and all the kings of Canaan would know that the GOD of Israel was fighting for His people.

In Mr. Armytage's picture, the Captain of the LORD's host appears as a warrior, armed with a sword and shield, and breastplate, but instead of a helmet there is a circlet of gold upon his head, and he wears a long cloak almost covering his bare feet. Joshua is taking off his sandals in obedience to the Captain's command. He wears a helmet, and there is a sword slung over his shoulder, and a quiver full of arrows on his back, and the edge of a round shield can be seen on his right hand. The moon is full, and it shines upon the face and figure of the Captain; but Joshua is in the shadow. Beyond him there are men asleep on the ground; and the strong walls of Jericho look white and cold in the bright moonlight.

THE ANGEL APPEARING TO JOSHUA.   E. ARMYTAGE, R.A., DEL^{T.}

THE FALL OF THE WALLS OF JERICHO.

The LORD told Joshua that all the men of war of the tribes of Israel were to march once round the City of Jericho every day for six days. Seven Priests, carrying seven trumpets of ram's horns, were to walk in front of the ark, which was to be borne aloft in the middle of the host. On the seventh day the army was to march round the city seven times; the Priests were to blow a long loud blast with their horns, and all the people were to shout with a great shout; and the walls of the city would fall down flat before them.

In the picture by Mr. Armstead, the Priests are blowing the loud blast with their trumpets of ram's horns; they wear their priestly robes of fine white linen, but instead of the mitre a long linen veil is thrown over their heads. In front of the Priests the men of war are shouting with a great shout; they carry spears and wear helmets and close fitting armour, which leaves their arms and legs bare. Joshua, who is riding upon a beautiful horse close to the ark, has a cloak thrown over his armour. The Priests who bare the ark have fallen upon their knees, and are leaning upon the poles of the ark. We can see the ring through which one pole is passed. The golden figure of an angel with outspread wings is lying upon the top of the ark. In the distance the walls of Jericho are falling into ruins at the sound of that loud blast and mighty shout from the army of Israel.

Joshua sent the two spies to fetch Rahab and her family, and bring them in safety to the camp; but the rest of the people were put to death and the city burnt with fire.

THE FALL OF THE WALLS OF JERICHO.　H. H. ARMSTEAD, R.A., DELT.

THE SUN AND MOON STAND STILL.

———

After the fall of Jericho five kings of Canaan gathered a great army together and fought with Joshua outside the city of Gibeon. The Israelites slew their enemies with great slaughter and chased them up a narrow pass over the heights of Bethhoron.

Joshua was afraid that the day would not be long enough for the Israelites to finish the battle, and he prayed unto the LORD to give them light that they might overtake all their enemies.

Then Joshua stood upon a hill in sight of the army of Israel, and cried,

"Sun, stand thou still upon Gibeon,
And thou Moon in the Valley of Ajalon."

And the sun stayed in the midst of heaven and hasted not to go down about a whole day.

In the picture by Mr. Armstead, Joshua is on horseback on the top of the cliffs, overhanging the plain of Gibeon; and he has stretched out his right hand towards the sun, which is low in the heavens. The three warriors on the cliff close to him are shooting arrows upon the Canaanites, as they rush up from the plain through the pass. Three of the kings, in chariots drawn by horses, lead the way. They are safer than the warriors on horseback, as they cannot easily be dragged out of their chariots; but one king has dropped the reins, and his horses are rushing madly on over some warriors who have fallen in the pass. Three men are trying to lift a wounded comrade, and one has raised his arm to warn a horseman not to trample upon them. The Canaanite warriors used swords, and one is holding up a strange shield in the form of an umbrella. In the plain below the cliffs, the sunshine is streaming upon the tents of the Canaanites, but we cannot see the city of Gibeon.

124

THE SUN AND MOON STAND STILL.   H. H. ARMSTEAD, R.A., DELᵀ.

THE FIVE KINGS HIDING IN THE CAVE.

The mountains were full of caves, and at Makkedah there was one larger than the rest. The five kings fled into it and hid themselves there. It was told Joshua that the five kings were hidden in the cave; and he commanded the warriors to roll great stones to the mouth of the cave and to set men to watch by it.

When the Israelites had pursued the Canaanites even to the gates of their cities, they returned to Makkedah to rest after a long day's battle. On the next morning Joshua ordered the five kings to be brought before him; and he commanded his captains to put their feet on the necks of the kings, saying, "Fear not; be strong and of good courage, for thus shall the LORD do to all your enemies against whom ye fight."

Mr. Dalziel has drawn a picture of the five kings hidden in the cave. They are all handsome men; and the one who wears no beard looks quite young. Two are talking earnestly together in the background; the younger is pointing his finger as if describing something to his aged comrade, who has clasped his hands together in astonishment at the tale. The young king is talking to an older man; they are both sitting down upon rocks, and perhaps they are trying to form some plan for escape. The fifth is lying fast asleep with his head resting against a rock. He looks more tired than the others. They all wear curious turbans of different shapes, and four have coats with sleeves. The background of the cave is dark, but there is strong light from some opening, and it falls upon the sleeping king.

The kings were slain with the sword, and their bodies hung upon trees round the cave.

THE FIVE KINGS HIDING IN THE CAVE.

E. G. DALZIEL, DELᵀ.

THE FEAST OF TABERNACLES.

Joshua divided the Land of Canaan amongst the twelve tribes of Israel, and during his lifetime he ruled over them. Shechem was their chief town, but the Tabernacle was set up at Shiloh. The Canaanites were not all driven out of the land; they had fled to their strongholds and often troubled the Israelites by sudden attacks.

Before his death Joshua warned the Israelites against worshipping the false gods of Canaan. He called the people together and spoke to them, saying, "The LORD is a holy GOD. He is a jealous GOD. If ye forsake Him and serve strange gods, then He will turn, and do you evil, and consume you, after that He hath done you good."

And the people answered, "Nay, but we will serve the LORD."

And Joshua wrote down their words in the book of the Law of GOD.

Now that the Israelites were settled in the land, they could keep the feasts which Moses had appointed.

Mr. S. Solomon has drawn a picture of the Feast of Tabernacles, which was kept in memory of the time when the people dwelt in tents in the wilderness. At the end of the harvest of corn, and of wine and oil, when the fields were all reaped, and the grapes and olives gathered, this feast was held. It was a very joyous time. The people lived in booths made of branches of pine, olive, myrtle, and palm-trees, put up in the courts and streets, and sometimes on the flat roofs of the houses; and there was much music and dancing, and the blowing of trumpets twenty-one times each day. In the picture the men are carrying citrons, and the house is decorated with green branches. The three men in white linen robes and mitres are priests; and the woman with the children is the wife of the eldest, who is kissing the High-Priest's hand.

THE FEAST OF TABERNACLES.   S. SOLOMON, Delt.

THE DEATH OF EGLON.

Some years after the death of Joshua, Eglon, a Prince of Moab, led a great army across the river Jordan and took Jericho, one of the cities belonging to the tribe of Benjamin. The people suffered much from the bands of armed men, who carried off all their fruit and corn; and they were forced to pay a tribute to Eglon.

When they cried unto the LORD in their distress, He raised up a deliverer to help them.

Ehud, one of the princes of Benjamin, a left-handed man, was chosen by his tribe to take the tribute to Eglon; he made a sword with two edges and hid it under his raiment upon his right thigh. After the tribute had been paid, he returned to the palace and sent a message to Eglon, saying, "I have a secret errand unto thee, O King." The King was sitting in a summer parlour, a cool, quiet room on the flat roof, and he sent for the young Benjamite to come to him there.

In the picture by Mr. Madox Brown the two men are alone. The King is sitting on a large chair with his feet raised upon a stool, and close to him there is a little table for wine. Eglon is a big fat man, with a black beard. There are bracelets on his great arms, and a heavy necklace upon his throat, and he wears a circlet of gold set with jewels. Ehud has just spoken the words, "I have a message from GOD unto thee," and Eglon is trying to rise in reverence to the GOD of Israel; in doing so he has knocked the table, and the cup and jar are falling from it. Ehud's left hand is drawing out the sword, hidden under his striped garment, and as the King rises he will thrust it into him. There is a lattice round the chamber to let in air and light. Painted figures and writing in curious characters can be seen round the dais and on the wall.

Ehud escaped from the chamber, and raising a great army, drove the Moabites out of the land.

THE DEATH OF EGLON.   F. MADOX BROWN, DELt.

GIDEON'S OFFERING CONSUMED BY FIRE.

————

The Children of Israel forsook the LORD their GOD and began to worship Baal ; and the LORD delivered them into the hands of the Midianites seven years. Every spring the Midianites crossed the Jordan, and pitching their tents in the great Plain of Jezreel, robbed the tribes of Canaan of their corn, and fruit, and cattle. The Israelites fled to the caves to hide themselves and lived there all summer. At last they cried unto the LORD to help them, and He raised up a leader and deliverer for His people.

The LORD sent an angel to Gideon, a young man of the tribe of Manasseh, to tell him that he must lead the Israelites against their enemies.

Gideon was threshing wheat near a cave, when the angel came to him with the message ; and he asked for a sign that it was really true. He went to his father's house, and made ready a kid and some cakes ; and he put the flesh in a basket and the broth in a pot, and brought them out to the man, who was sitting under an oak tree. The angel told Gideon to lay the food upon a rock and pour the broth over it ; and Gideon did so. Then the angel putting forth the staff that was in his hand, touched the offering ; and there went up fire out of the rock and consumed the flesh and cakes ; and the angel departed out of Gideon's sight.

In the picture by Mr. Dalziel young Gideon is kneeling on the ground, watching the angel ascend up to Heaven in the smoke of his sacrifice. The angel wears a beautiful robe, fastened with a jewel, and there are bracelets on his bare arms. He holds the staff in his left hand and has raised the right, as if to remind Gideon that the sign has been granted to him ; and Gideon knows that he must obey the voice of the angel. The basket and the pot are lying upon the ground near a great oak tree ; and the huts belonging to Gideon's father can be seen in the field beyond. The LORD was with Gideon ; the young Israelite raised a great army and drove the Midianites out of the land. And Gideon judged Israel for many years.

GIDEON'S OFFERING CONSUMED BY FIRE.

SAMSON AND THE LION.

Again the Israelites did evil in the sight of the Lord; and the Lord delivered them into the hands of the Philistines; but, at the end of forty years, he raised up a man of great strength and courage to fight for them.

Samson was a Nazarite from his birth; he was under a vow never to cut his hair and never to drink wine; and when still a youth, the Spirit of the Lord began to move him to hot anger against the Philistines.

But he loved a Philistine maiden of Timnath, and used to go and visit her; and one day, on the way down the slopes of the hills to the flat plain of the Philistines, a lion met him in the road. Samson rent the lion, as he would have rent a kid, and flung him down upon the ground.

In Sir Frederick Leighton's picture the lion has met Samson in a narrow pass between vineyards. The young man carries no weapon in his hand, for he had meant to travel quietly on the high road with his old parents. He has caught the lion by the mane and crushed him against the wall. The lion is lifted up from the ground, and his claw is fast in Samson's robe. At that moment, perhaps for the first time, Samson learnt what mighty strength lay in his young arms; and it was given to him that he might fight against the enemies of Israel. We cannot see Samson's face, only the curly golden hair which had never been cut. Samson means strong and sunny.

Samson soon quarrelled with his wife's family, and beginning to fight single-handed against the Philistines, killed thirty men one day. Afterwards he set fire to the corn on the plain, and three thousand Philistines came to bind him; but he broke their cords asunder, and, seizing the jawbone of an ass, killed a thousand of his enemies.

SAMSON AND THE LION.   SIR FREDK. LEIGHTON, P.R.A., DELᵀ.

SAMSON CARRYING THE GATES.

When Samson went down to Gaza, a stronghold of the Philistines, he saw there a woman whom he loved, and stayed with her, until after the gates were shut for the night. The Philistines knew where he was; and they meant to go to the house and kill their enemy as soon as it was daylight.

But at midnight Samson arose, and laying hold of the doors of the gate of the city and the two posts, plucked them up, bar and all; and putting them upon his shoulders carried the burden to the top of a mountain.

In the picture by Sir Frederick Leighton, Samson has just laid the heavy gates and the posts upon his shoulders, and is carrying them off. His face is hidden in the shadow of the burden, but we can see the long cloak thrown over his head and back. It is night; the stars are shining clearly in the dark sky; and the walls and towers of Gaza are gleaming white in the moonlight.

This time Samson used his great strength for his own pleasure, not in fighting the enemies of the LORD. His faith was very different from the loving faith of Moses and Joshua; it did not make his life pure and good. Samson was not a leader of Israel; he was simply a mighty man of valour who was under the vow of a Nazarite to spend his strength in smiting down the enemies of the GOD of Israel.

SAMSON CARRYING THE GATES.   SIR FREDK. LEIGHTON, P.R.A., DELᵀ.

SAMSON AT THE MILL.

———

Afterwards Samson loved another Philistine woman, named Delilah; and the lords of the Philistines promised to give her a great sum of money, if she could persuade Samson to tell her wherein his great strength lay.

For some time Samson would not speak the truth to Delilah; but at last the woman urged him so strongly that he told his secret: "If I be shaven, then my strength will go from me, and I shall become weak and be like any other man."

The next time Samson came to see Delilah, she made him go to sleep with his head upon her knees, and called for a man who was near at hand to shave off the seven locks of his hair. When Samson awoke, he found that his strength was gone from him. The Philistines laid hold upon their enemy and put out his eyes; and bringing the blind captive down to Gaza, they set him to grind corn in the prison-house.

In the picture by Sir Frederick Leighton, Samson is sitting on the stone base of the mill. He has been walking round and round grinding the corn, and has stopped to rest for a moment. The Philistine keeper has rushed in with a stick to beat the blind prisoner, and make him go on with his task. Samson has bent his head, and looks as if he had not heard the keeper come in; but the man's blow will soon rouse him. Samson's hair is beginning to grow again, and with it his mighty strength will return.

After a few weeks, the lords of the Philistines sent for Samson to make sport for them, as they sat at a feast in the temple of their god, Dagon. Samson cried to the LORD to strengthen him that he might be avenged for his two eyes; and he leaned with all his might upon a pillar of the temple until it broke. The roof fell in upon the crowd; and they were all killed together.

SAMSON AT THE MILL.   SIR FREDK. LEIGHTON, P.R.A., DELT.

RUTH AND NAOMI.

During several years there was a famine in the Land of Canaan. Very little rain fell; and the corn and grass would not grow in the hard dry ground. A man of Bethlehem, called Elimelech, took his flocks and herds across the Jordan, and settled in the Land of Moab; but he died very soon, leaving a widow and two sons. The two sons married Moabite women, and died also, leaving no children. Then the widow, Naomi, made up her mind to return to Bethlehem. The little family had grown very poor; there was nothing left for Naomi to take with her; and she started on foot to walk to Bethlehem to seek shelter there. Her two daughters-in-law, Orpah and Ruth, who were to return to their own mother's homes, went some way with her.

In Mr. Solomon's picture Naomi has just parted with Orpah, and is trying to persuade Ruth to follow her sister-in-law. Ruth has clasped Naomi's hand in hers and is speaking earnestly: "Intreat me not to leave thee, nor to return from following after thee; whither thou goest I will go; where thou lodgest I will lodge; thy people shall be my people; and thy GOD, my GOD." Ruth is very beautiful, and she is gazing tenderly into Naomi's face; and Naomi sees that her dear daughter-in-law would rather share her poverty than be married to another husband in the Land of Moab. The young widows wear long white veils tied over their heads, and long loose white garments. Naomi and Ruth are standing at the end of the road; below them lies the Jordan; they will cross the river together; and Ruth will go to Bethlehem and be a comfort to the lonely old widow.

RUTH AND NAOMI. S. SOLOMON, DELᵀ

NAOMI AND THE CHILD OBED.

Naomi and Ruth were very poor; and Ruth said to her mother-in-law, "Let me go now into the fields and glean among the ears of corn." Naomi answered, "Go, my daughter." Now it chanced that Ruth came to the field of Boaz, a rich kinsman of Elimelech. He had not been told of Naomi's return, and noticing the beautiful young widow, asked who she was. When he heard the story of her kindness to Naomi, he made up his mind to be a friend to them both.

There was a law in Israel that when a man died, leaving no children, his nearest kinsman was to marry the widow, and the first son of the second marriage was to have the name and lands of the first husband.

Boaz asked the nearest kinsman of Elimelech's sons if he wished to marry Ruth, and when the man seemed unwilling, Boaz took her himself for a wife, and brought Naomi home to live with them.

Boaz was a good man, and he loved his young wife dearly; they had a little son called Obed. In the picture by Mr. Solomon, the boy is in Naomi's arms; it will inherit her husband's name and lands. Naomi has laid her hand on Ruth's head in a loving caress, and is gazing tenderly at her little grandson; in her great love for this young mother and child all the sorrows of the past are forgotten, and she is quite happy again. Ruth is also very happy with her husband and child; she is rewarded for all her goodness to Naomi. There are beautiful lilies in a vase on the table, and some more at the window. Boaz is a rich man, and we can imagine that his gentle young wife will rule her household with kindness.

NAOMI AND THE CHILD OBED.   S. SOLOMON, DELᵀ

SAMUEL AND HIS MOTHER.

In the days of Eli, the High Priest, GOD raised up a prophet to teach His people and turn them from their evil ways. Samuel was the son of Elkanah, a man of the tribe of Ephraim. His mother, Hannah, had vowed a vow unto the LORD that, if he would give her a son, the child should be a Nazarite from his birth; he should belong to GOD all his life long.

When the boy was three years old, Elkanah and Hannah took him up to Shiloh to be a little servant to Eli, the High Priest. Samuel could not be a priest himself, because he was not of the tribe of Levi; but in later days all Israel obeyed him as being above king or priest; they looked upon him as a prophet who pleaded with GOD for them; and Samuel taught them that they must be kind and truthful, and pure in heart, if they would draw near to GOD in prayer.

In Mr. Armstead's picture Samuel is still a child. His father and mother used to see him every Spring, when they came up to Shiloh to offer the yearly sacrifice, and Hannah always brought her son a little coat. Samuel was with Eli when they came in, and he has run forward to receive his mother's kiss. He has a beautiful face, and his bright hair is quite long; it will never be cut. When he turns to his father, he will notice the new robe upon his arm; and his mother will put it on over his white linen gown to see if it is long enough. Her boy grows very much from year to year. Hannah's hair is long and curly; she has a cloak thrown over her head and covering her figure. The old High Priest does not wear all his priestly robes; this is a friendly visit, and he will talk to the parents of their little son and tell them how good he is.

H. H. ARMSTEAD, R.A., DEL.ᵀ

SAMUEL AND HIS MOTHER

SAMUEL AND ELI.

Eli had two very wicked sons; and the LORD sent a prophet to tell him that the High Priesthood would be taken from his family because of their sins; but the men would not listen to their father's warning words, and went on doing evil in the sight of the LORD.

Then GOD sent another message by Samuel. One night the boy heard a voice calling "Samuel"; and he ran to see if the High Priest wanted something; but Eli had not called him. Again a voice called "Samuel," and the child got up once more to run to the old High Priest. Eli sent him back to bed; and in a very short time the voice called again "Samuel!" Then Eli told the boy to go and lie down, and if he heard the voice again to answer, "Speak LORD, for Thy servant heareth."

The LORD GOD told Samuel that trouble was coming upon Eli and upon the House of Aaron, because the High Priest had not punished his sons in their youth, and forced them to give up their wicked ways.

Samuel did not like to take these dreadful tidings to Eli; he waited until the old man sent for him, and told him not to hide anything that he had heard from the LORD.

In the picture by Mr. Armstead the child has raised his hands and is repeating, word for word, what he had heard in the night; he is keeping nothing back, although he loves the High Priest and cannot bear to grieve him. Eli is sitting with bent head and open hands, receiving the evil tidings with heart-broken humility, saying only, "It is the LORD; let Him do what seemeth Him good." They are in one of the rooms built near the Tabernacle for the use of the priests; the walls are hung with embroidered curtains, and Eli is upon a low seat with a carved back.

146

H. H. ARMSTEAD, R.A., DEL.ᵀ

SAMUEL AND ELI.

"AND DAVID TOOK AN HARP."

Mr. Solomon has drawn a picture of Saul, the first King of Israel. He had been anointed king by Samuel, and so long as he obeyed the prophet who spoke in the name of the LORD, all went well with him. But in later life Saul was separated from GOD and His prophet through his own disobedience; and an evil spirit from the LORD troubled him, driving him nearly mad with melancholy.

Saul knew that GOD had chosen a man after His own heart to reign over His people; and he was in constant fear of being driven from the throne.

He heard of a young shepherd, named David, who could play sweetly upon the harp, and, hoping that music would soothe his troubled heart and brain, he sent for the boy to come and play to him.

Saul's face is very dark and sad, and he has clasped his hands tightly together. There is a bracelet upon his arm, but his robe is quite plain, and he is sitting upon a plain chair. He does not know yet that this young David is to be the king after GOD's own heart; and he loves the boy dearly; his music drives away the evil spirit for a time.

David was a poet, and could sing beautiful psalms to the music of the harp; and he was so simple and loving that his companionship cheered the unhappy king. He was the great grandson of Boaz and Ruth.

In the picture David's face is turned to the king; he is watching to see if the music has any effect upon his master. He is dressed very simply with a girdle round his short robe. His hair is rather long, but he is not a Nazarite. His harp is small and curiously shaped.

S. SOLOMON, DELT.

"AND DAVID TOOK AN HARP."

CUSHI BRINGS TO DAVID NEWS OF THE DEATH OF ABSALOM.

After Saul's death David was King of Israel for many years. The LORD was with him, and gave him the victory over all his enemies. The twelve tribes of Israel were united into one kingdom now; and the Canaanites were driven out of the land.

A great sorrow came upon David in later life. His son Absalom rebelled against him, and raising a great army, took possession of Jerusalem. David was forced to fly from the city and take refuge across the Jordan; but his warriors rallied round him, and went out to meet Absalom in battle. Although David had commanded the captains to spare the young man's life, he was sorely afraid lest Absalom should fall, and waited all day long in the stronghold of Mahanaim for news.

Mr. Small has drawn a picture of David at the moment when a messenger has arrived from the field of battle. The king is covered with a dark cloak thrown over his white linen robe, and a sword hangs at his side; but he wears no bracelets nor jewels of any kind. His hair and beard are long; and his eyes are bent upon the ground. The messenger has been running for hours, and is pressing one hand to his side, trying to get breath to speak. "Is the young man, Absalom, safe?" asks the king; and Cushi answers, "May all the enemies of my Lord the King be as that young man." David understands what he means. Absalom is dead. The servants and warriors, listening in the portico, know how dearly the king loved his son, and they are watching to see how he will take the news.

David turned slowly round, to go up to a chamber above the gates, and as he went, he cried, "Oh, my son Absalom! my son, my son Absalom! would GOD I had died for thee. O! Absalom, my son, my son!"

150

CUSHI BRINGS TO DAVID NEWS OF THE DEATH OF ABSALOM.   W. SMALL, DELT.

HOSANNAH!

After David's death, his son, Solomon, reigned over the tribes of Israel. GOD gave him wisdom, and great riches and honour; and in his days, the little kingdom of Israel held a high place amongst the nations.

Solomon built a beautiful temple at Jerusalem, upon Mount Moriah. The Ark and the Golden Altar, and the Table for shew-bread, which had been kept in the Tabernacle, were brought to the Temple, and the old Tabernacle itself was stored up there. From this time Jerusalem was the Holy City; the High Priest lived there, and all the people came up to offer sacrifices at the feasts.

While the priests offered the sacrifices, the Levites sang to the music of their harps, and every day, morning and evening, a beautiful service was held in the courts of the Temple.

Mr. Solomon has drawn a picture of a young Levite, playing upon his harp in one of the courts of the Temple. The harp is of a curious shape, ornamented with a fringe, and the musician is holding it firmly with his right hand, while playing with the left. He has a beautiful face, and is listening to the sweet sounds of the instrument, as if he loved to hear them. A striped scarf with a fringe is twisted over his linen ephod, and he wears a striped turban. There is a curtain against the wall of the court, and branches of trees can be seen above it. "Hosannah in Excelsis," is the form in which our "Glory to GOD in the Highest," appears in Christian worship, when Latin was always used in the services.

HOSANNAH!   S. SOLOMON, DEL^T.

ELIJAH FED BY RAVENS.

The prophet Elijah lived in the reign of Ahab, King of Israel. Ahab did that which was evil in the sight of the LORD above all the kings that were before him. He took to wife Jezebel, a daughter of the heathen King of the Zidonians, and he served their god Baal, and worshipped him. And he reared up an altar for Baal in the house of Baal, which he had built in Samaria; and he provoked the LORD to anger.

Then Elijah the prophet came to Ahab and said, "As the LORD, the GOD of Israel, liveth, before whom I stand, there shall not be dew nor rain these years but according to my word."

Afterwards the word of the LORD came unto Elijah, saying, "Get thee hence, and hide thyself by the brook Cherith. Thou shalt drink of the brook, and I have commanded the ravens to feed thee there."

And the ravens brought Elijah bread and flesh in the morning, and bread and flesh in the evening, and he drank of the brook.

Mr. Walker has drawn a picture of Elijah sitting by the brook. His long hair and beard make him look very wild, and he wears nothing but the skin of some animal round his loins. The prophet's life is spent in the deserts; and it is in these lonely places, far away from cities, that he hears the Voice of GOD. The ravens are flying about him, and he is taking a piece of bread from one.

There was no rain in the land of Canaan for three years; the ground was baked dry by the hot sun, and the corn and grass failed. Ahab sent messengers to all the neighbouring kingdoms seeking for the prophet. If no rain came the people would all perish in the famine; and the king wanted Elijah to save the land from ruin.

154

ELIJAH FED BY RAVENS.

F. S. WALKER, RHA, DELT.

ELIJAH AND THE WIDOW'S SON.

When the brook Cherith dried up, the Lord said to Elijah, "Arise, get thee to Zarephath; I have commanded a widow woman there to sustain thee."

The prophet arose, and coming to the gate of the city, he saw a widow woman gathering sticks, and asked her to fetch him a little water and a morsel of bread. The woman answered that she had no food left but a little meal and oil; she was gathering a few sticks to bake a cake for herself and her son that they might eat it and die. And Elijah said to her, "Fear not; for thus saith the Lord God of Israel, The barrel of meal shall not waste, neither shall the cruise of oil fail, until the day that the Lord sendeth rain upon the earth."

Elijah went to live in a chamber at the widow's house; and there was always enough meal and oil to make cakes for the little family.

It came to pass that the woman's son died, and she was in sore distress.

Elijah took the boy out of her arms, and carrying him upstairs, laid him upon his own bed. And he stretched himself upon the body three times, and cried unto the Lord to let the child's soul come unto him again, and the Lord hearkened unto the prayer of Elijah, and the child revived.

Mr. Madox Brown has drawn a picture of Elijah carrying the boy down to his mother. The prophet wears a long, fringed robe and cloak, and there are sandals upon his feet. For the last few months he has been living in a city, and is obliged to dress like other people. The boy is in grave-clothes, bound round and round with bands of ribbon; he could not have walked downstairs. The mother has knelt down before Elijah, and has raised her clasped hands, saying, "Now I know that thou art a man of God, and the word of the Lord in thy mouth is truth." The staircase is outside the house, and we can see the door of Elijah's room.

156

ELIJAH AND THE WIDOW'S SON.   F. MADOX BROWN, DEL^T

THE ARROW OF DELIVERANCE.

As a young man, Elisha has been a servant to Elijah; and after his master's translation into Heaven, he became known as a prophet of the LORD. He lived in Samaria; and when the kings of Israel provoked the LORD to anger by their evil ways, and were in great distress because of the inroads of the Syrians, Elisha cried unto the LORD to forgive them and help them.

When the prophet was very old, and sick unto death, Joash, the young king of Israel, came down to his house to weep over him; and he cried, "My father, my father, the chariot of Israel and the horsemen thereof!" The king believed that the prophet of the LORD had been the defender of Israel, and after his death there would be no one left to cry to the GOD of Israel for help against the Syrians.

Elisha said unto him, "Take thy bow and arrows"; and the prophet laid his hand upon the king's hand. And he said, "Open the window eastward"; and the king opened it. Then said Elisha, "Shoot"; and he shot. Elisha told Joash that his arrow was the LORD's arrow of victory over Syria; the king should smite the Syrians until they were consumed. He commanded Joash to shoot again out of the window upon the ground. Joash shot three arrows; and the prophet said, he should smite the Syrians three times.

In the picture by Mr. Murch the king is using a large bow and his arrow has a sharp point. He wears a helmet set with jewels, and there is a heavy bracelet upon his arm. His armour is formed of narrow bands of metal fastened over his fringed robe, which falls just below the knee. A dagger with a beautiful hilt is thrust into one band. Elisha is covered up with a large blanket, and is leaning back on a low chair. Water and food are lying on the little table near him.

158

THE ARROW OF DELIVERANCE.

A. MURCH, DEL^T.

THE FLIGHT OF ADRAMMELECH.

In the reign of Hezekiah, king of Judah, Sennacherib, the king of Assyria, took all the strongholds of Judah. Hezekiah was obliged to pay him a tribute of money, and to give up all the silver and gold that could be found in the Temple.

Soon afterwards Sennacherib sent a large army to take Jerusalem; but the LORD heard the prayers of Hezekiah, and commanded the prophet Isaiah to tell the king that He would defend Jerusalem.

And it came to pass that night, that the Angel of the LORD went forth and smote in the camp of the Assyrians 185,000 men; and Sennacherib was obliged to return to Nineveh with the remnant of his army. When he was worshipping in the temple of Nisroch, his god, his sons, Adrammelech and Sharezer, smote him with the sword; and they fled and escaped into the Land of Ararat.

In the picture by Mr. Murch the two sons are making haste to escape out of the temple, before anyone comes in and finds their father lying dead upon the ground.

Adrammelech is in armour; he wears a helmet and coat-of-mail; and over all a loose garment which is flying behind him. Sharezer is looking back at the figure of the king, lying upon the pavement. It is a splendid temple, adorned with curious figures, carved and painted upon the walls, and there are two enormous figures of strange-looking animals. A tame eagle can be seen taking food out of a dish upon the pavement. Nisroch means "the great eagle," and amongst the ruins of Nineveh there are eagle-headed human figures fighting with lions and bulls. Behind the eagle stands a small altar for incense, and another on the other side.

THE FLIGHT OF ADRAMMELECH.

A. MURCH, DELt.

JONAH CAST INTO THE SEA.

The prophet Jonah lived in the days of Jeroboam II., King of Israel. The LORD GOD commanded him to go to Nineveh to warn the people that the city would be destroyed because of their great wickedness.

Jonah did not wish to go to the great heathen city; and he rose up to flee from the presence of the LORD. He went down to Joppa, and finding a ship ready to sail for Tarshish, he paid the fare and went on board.

The LORD sent a great wind, and there was a mighty tempest in the sea so that the ship was like to be broken. The sailors were afraid and cried, every man unto his GOD. But Jonah had gone down into the innermost parts of the ship, and was fast asleep, until the shipmaster awoke him roughly, bidding him cry upon his GOD. The sailors believed that the tempest had come upon them because of the wickedness of someone on board, and they cast lots to see who was the evil doer.

The lot fell upon Jonah; and he confessed that he had fled from the presence of the LORD. He said, "Take me up and cast me forth into the sea, so shall the sea be calm unto you, for I know that for my sake this great tempest is upon you."

In Mr. Dalziel's picture the sailors have just thrown Jonah into the sea. They do not like to obey his command, and are frightened when the sea grows calmer as Jonah sinks below the waves. Two or three of the men are negroes; they pull at the great oars which can be seen at the side of the vessel, but there are ropes for sails when the wind is favourable.

The LORD had prepared a great fish to swallow up Jonah; and he remained inside the fish for three days and three nights; then it threw him out upon the dry land.

The men of Nineveh repented at the preaching of Jonah; and the LORD spared the city.

162

JONAH CAST INTO THE SEA.   T. DALZIEL, DELT.

JOB RECEIVING THE MESSENGERS.

There was a man in the land of Uz whose name was Job, and the man was perfect and upright, one that feared GOD and hated evil. He had seven sons and three daughters, and he was rich in cattle, and had a very great household.

And the LORD GOD tried His servant Job with many afflictions, to see if he would remain steadfast in his faith in Him.

One day a messenger arrived to tell Job that the Sabeans had carried off his oxen and his asses, and had slain his servants; and while he was yet speaking, there came another servant who brought news of the destruction of the sheep and shepherds by fire; and in the same hour, a third arrived to bring his master word that the Chaldeans had fallen upon the camels and slain their drivers. While he was yet speaking, there came another messenger with still worse news. Job's sons and daughters were holding a feast in the eldest brother's house, when a great wind smote the four corners of the house, and it fell upon the young people and killed them. Job was in sore distress, but he would not doubt the goodness of the LORD; he said, "The LORD gave and the LORD hath taken away, blessed be the name of the LORD."

A dreadful sickness came upon Job, yet still he would not doubt the goodness of the LORD. His friends tried to make him believe that he was being punished for sin, but Job was quite sure that his sufferings were not sent as a punishment; they did not separate him from GOD, who still loved him.

Mr. Small has drawn a picture of Job in the dreadful hour when the servants arrived with evil tidings. The last has just run in with the news of his children's death, and Job looks as if he could not believe the man's words. The other men are horrified, and Job's wife has clasped her hands before her face.

After many days, the LORD rewarded His servant by giving him more children and twice as much wealth as he had before.

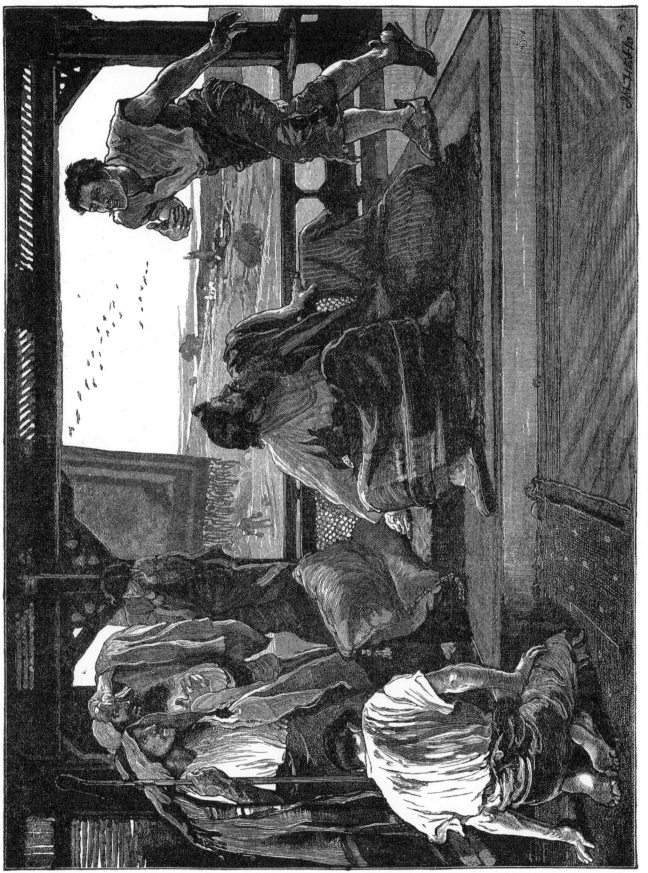

W. SMALL, DELT.

JOB RECEIVING THE MESSENGERS.

JEWISH WOMEN BURNING INCENSE.— JEREMIAH.

———

The Prophet Jeremiah was the son of Hilkiah, a priest, and lived at Anathoth, near Jerusalem. He had no wife nor child, and spent all his life in preaching against the folly and wickedness of the people of Jerusalem, and in warning them of the hopeless ruin they were bringing upon their country.

The Prophet lived to see the people carried away to Babylon; but he did not go into captivity himself. He found favour with Nebuchadnezzar, and was allowed to remain in Judæa. Jeremiah prophesied that the Israelites would return to their own land after seventy years' captivity, when every man would take possession of the fields and vineyards belonging to his family.

Some of the people had taken refuge in Egypt; and Jeremiah either went there himself, or sent a message from God to warn them against their evil doings. He had heard that the Jewish women still burnt incense to a false goddess, whom they called queen of heaven. They had burnt incense and poured out drink-offerings to her in Jerusalem; and in spite of the awful punishment which had come upon them because of idolatry, they went on sinning against the Lord, and would not hearken to Jeremiah's warnings.

In the picture by Mr. Solomon, the women are standing in a court. Two of them are mixing incense with a spoon before setting fire to it; and another in the distance is holding up a small basin, and is about to pour out a drink-offering; and there is a child playing upon a harp. They are beautiful women, and their dark hair is carefully arranged and ornamented with leaves. They wear bracelets and white flowing robes, and are evidently women of the upper class, who set a bad example to their poor neighbours.

166

S. SOLOMON, DEL^{T.}

JEWISH WOMEN BURNING INCENSE.—JEREMIAH.

THE PARABLE OF THE BOILING POT.

The Prophet Ezekiel was a native of Jerusalem, and of a priestly family. When still young, he was carried captive to Babylon with King Jehoiachin and other Jews of noble birth, very soon after the Temple had been plundered by Nebuchadnezzar. He settled with his family on the banks of the river Chebar, two hundred miles north of Babylon; and his house became a meeting-place for all faithful Israelites who mourned over their exile.

Sir E. Burne-Jones has drawn a picture of Ezekiel's parable of the boiling pot. It was uttered upon a day when Nebuchadnezzar had drawn near to Jerusalem to take it. Ezekiel cried: "Thus saith the LORD, set on the caldron and pour water into it; gather the pieces thereof into it, even every good piece, the thigh and the shoulder; fill it with choice bones. Heap on the wood; make the fire hot; boil well the flesh. Then set it empty upon the coals thereof, that it may be hot, and that the filthiness and the rust of it may be consumed."

The Prophet meant, that everything of any value in Jerusalem would be destroyed by Nebuchadnezzar, and the city itself, like the empty caldron, would be purified by fire.

In the picture, the Prophet is stirring up the flesh and bones, and adding more wood to the fire to make the broth boil quickly. His thoughts are fixed upon his work, and he is paying no heed to the group of women, who are drinking wine and talking together in the distance. They wear garlands of flowers upon their heads; and one is lying upon a couch; Ezekiel's warnings have not roused them to a sense of danger; they are enjoying themselves idly, and do not notice what he is doing.

THE PARABLE OF THE BOILING POT.

BY THE RIVERS OF BABYLON.

During their exile in Babylon, the Jews learned to hate idols, and to trust in Jehovah, the GOD of their fathers. Ezekiel, the Prophet of the Exile, taught them that the captivity was a punishment for the sin of idolatry, and if they would turn to the LORD with all their hearts, He would have mercy upon them.

One of the Psalms of the Exile expresses their sadness:

"By the waters of Babylon we sat down and wept, when we remembered thee, O Sion.
"As for our harps, we hanged them up, upon the trees that are therein.
"For they that led us away captive required of us then a song, and melody in our heaviness;
"Sing us one of the songs of Sion.
"How shall we sing the Lord's song, in a strange land?"

Mr. Poynter has drawn a picture on the words of the Psalmist. Three Babylonians are trying to persuade the beautiful Jewish women to sing; they are taking their harps down from the willow-trees, and one man is stooping forward to speak to two of the captives. The women look very sorrowful and are clinging to each other for comfort and support; and one is asking, "How shall we sing the Lord's song in a strange land?" They wear long flowing robes and bracelets, and one woman, who is lying down upon a rug, has an ornament upon her head. The Babylonians loved bright colours and splendid garments, and these three men are richly dressed; their turbans are adorned with jewels, and their robes with fringes and embroidery. The company are assembled in a courtyard, built on the edge of the river, where water-lilies are growing; and we can see into a splendid hall. These captives are probably of noble birth, and have no hardships to bear; but they cannot be happy in exile.

BY THE RIVERS OF BABYLON.　　　　E. J. POYNTER, R A., DELᵀ·

THE CHRONICLES BEING READ TO THE KING.

In the time of the exile there were a number of Jews in Persia, and amongst them Mordecai, an officer of the court at Shushan. He had brought up a young cousin, called Esther. The girl was very beautiful, and the king chose her from amongst a number of maidens to be his queen. Mordecai charged Esther not to speak of her Jewish birth; and she obeyed him in all things. Soon afterwards Mordecai heard that two of the king's servants meant to kill their master; and he commanded Esther to go to King Ahasuerus and tell him of the plot. And it was written in the book of the Chronicles that Mordecai had saved the king's life.

Just at this time Ahasuerus raised Haman to power, who hated Mordecai, and was determined to destroy him with all the Jews in Persia.

In Mr. Houghton's picture the king is lying upon a couch. He cannot go to sleep, and has commanded that the book of the Chronicles should be brought and read aloud to him. The reader has just come to the place where it was written that Mordecai saved the king's life, and the king has raised his hand to ask, "What honour and dignity hath been done to Mordecai for this?" The reader is answering, "There is nothing done for him." A slave, who is hidden by the reader's figure, is pouring some cool liquid over the king's feet into a bason, and another young slave is holding up the scroll upon which the Chronicles are written. There are three officers of the court in the room, and they look jealous of the king's interest in Mordecai. The room is lighted by a lamp; two women are standing near it and a child with a fan of feathers.

Ahasuerus sent for Haman, and commanded him to clothe Mordecai in royal robes, and to lead the Jew on horseback through the city, proclaiming, "Thus shall it be done to the man whom the king delighteth to honour."

172

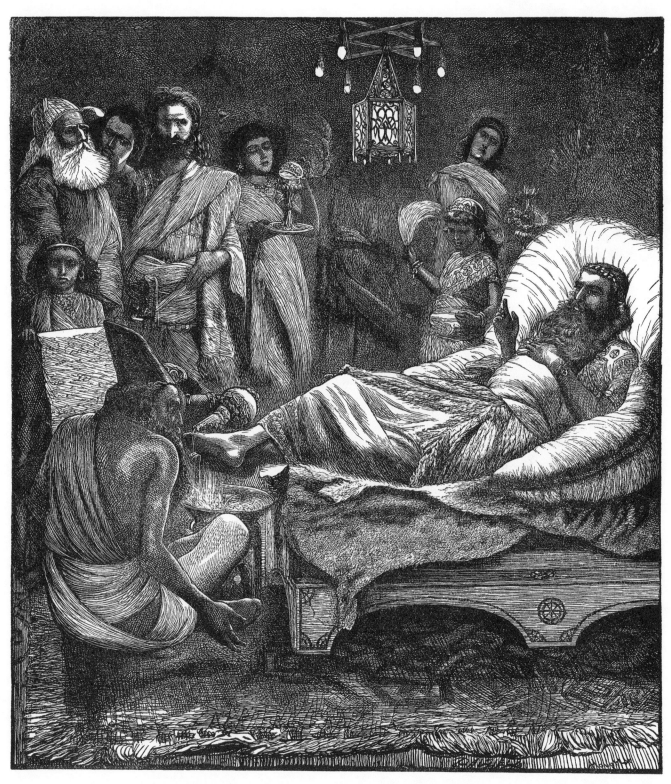

THE CHRONICLES BEING READ TO THE KING.   A. B. HOUGHTON, DELT.

ESTHER DENOUNCING HAMAN.

———

Haman had persuaded Ahasuerus to sign a decree, ordering all the Jews to be destroyed upon a certain day; and Mordecai told Esther that she must go to the king and ask him to spare her people. Esther was very much frightened lest the king should be angry at her boldness, but she could not let her people perish without trying to save them.

She invited the king and Haman to a banquet of wine, and during the banquet Ahasuerus, who knew that the young queen had a favour to ask, promised that her request should be granted, whatever it was. Esther took courage, and told Ahasuerus that all her people were to be destroyed. When the king heard that his beautiful young queen was of Jewish birth, he was very angry with Haman, and arose in wrath from the table to walk about in the garden.

In Mr. Brewtnall's picture the king has just come into the room again, to find that Haman has fallen down upon his knees before Esther. He is begging her to intercede for him. The king is exceedingly angry with Haman for daring to approach the queen; and Esther has lifted her arm and refused to listen to him. Esther is very beautiful. She wears a bracelet and a circlet of gold set with jewels, but her dress is dark and plain, perhaps because she is mourning over the sorrows of her people. Two slaves stand behind Esther's couch to fan her; there is no one else in the room. It is a summer-parlour built in the gardens.

Haman was hanged upon the gallows which he had prepared for Mordecai, and Mordecai was raised to great honour. The people in the city of Shushan rejoiced greatly; and the Jews had light and gladness, and joy and honour.

ESTHER DENOUNCING HAMAN.　　　E. F. BREWTNALL, DELT.

DANIEL'S PRAYER.

Daniel was carried away to Babylon in the reign of Jehoiakim, and being a handsome and clever boy of noble birth, he was chosen with three others to be trained for the service of the king. He remained a faithful Israelite, and, in answer to his prayer, GOD gave him power to interpret a dream which troubled King Nebuchadnezzar. From that day he rose step by step to a high position at the court, and was held in honour by Nebuchadnezzar above all the wise men in the country.

When Cyrus the Persian took Babylon, Darius the Mede received the kingdom, and in his days Daniel still held the highest place at court.

The other officers were jealous of the Jew, and they persuaded Darius to make a decree, that any man who prayed to any god, for thirty days, save only to the king himself, should be cast into the den of lions.

Daniel always kneeled upon his knees three times a day, in front of the windows of his chamber, which were open towards Jerusalem, and gave thanks to his GOD; and in Mr. Poynter's picture we see him, bent low in deep humility before the GOD of Israel. It is mid-day, and the sunshine is streaming upon his figure; his head is covered, but he has taken off his sandals and spread out his hands before the LORD. The walls of the chamber are beautifully carved, and there is a handsome carpet on the polished floor. The jealous officers are on the watch, and one has drawn back a curtain, and is pointing to Daniel; he will make haste to accuse him to the king.

Darius could not change his decree, and Daniel was cast into the den of lions; but GOD shut their mouths, and they did not hurt His faithful servant.

176

DANIEL'S PRAYER.

E. J. POYNTER, R.A., DELT.

SHADRACH, MESHACH, AND ABEDNEGO.

Shadrach, Meshach, and Abednego were educated with Daniel, and at Daniel's request Nebuchadnezzar gave them honourable places in the province of Babylon. About this time Nebuchadnezzar made an image of gold and set it up in the plain of Dura, near Babylon, and he commanded all his officers to come to the dedication of the image. At the sound of loud music they were to fall down and worship this new god, and whosoever refused to worship the image would be cast into the midst of a burning fiery furnace.

On the day of the dedication of the image, the king's officers noticed that the three Jews did not fall down at the sound of the loud music, neither did they worship the image; and they came and told Nebuchadnezzar. In answer to the king's questions, the men spoke out boldly. "O Nebuchadnezzar, we have no need to answer thee in this matter. If it be so, our GOD whom we serve is able to deliver us from the burning fiery furnace, and He will deliver us out of thine hand, O King. But if not, be it known unto thee, O King, that we will not serve thy gods, nor worship the golden image which thou hast set up."

Then Nebuchadnezzar, in his rage and fury, commanded that the men should be bound in their clothes and cast into the fire.

A little later, the king told his servants that he saw four men loose, walking in the midst of the fire, and the form of the fourth was like a son of the gods. And he called to Shadrach, Meshach, and Abednego, to come out of the furnace; and the three men came out unhurt; the fire had not touched them.

Mr. Solomon has drawn a picture of the three Jews, protected by the angel; his wings shield them from the fire; and they are standing unhurt and untroubled in the midst of the furnace. The peace of perfect faith in GOD rests upon their faces.

178

S. SOLOMON, DEL^T.

SHADRACH, MESHACH, AND ABEDNEGO.

ART PICTURES

FROM THE

OLD TESTAMENT

AND

OUR LORD'S PARABLES.

———————

PART II.

THE SOWER.

Behold a sower went forth to sow;

And when he sowed, some seeds fell by the way side, and the fowls came and devoured them up :

Some fell upon stony places, where they had not much earth : and forthwith they sprung up, because they had no deepness of earth :

And when the sun was up, they were scorched; and because they had no root, they withered away.

And some fell among thorns; and the thorns sprung up, and choked them :

But other fell into good ground, and brought forth fruit, some an hundredfold, some sixtyfold, some thirtyfold.

Who hath ears to hear, let him hear.

.   .   .   .   .   .

Hear ye therefore the parable of the sower.

When any one heareth the word of the kingdom, and understandeth it not, then cometh the wicked one, and catcheth away that which was sown in his heart.   This is he which received seed by the way side.

But he that received the seed into stony places, the same is he that heareth the word, and anon with joy receiveth it;

Yet hath he not root in himself, but dureth for a while : for when tribulation or persecution ariseth because of the word, by and by he is offended.

He also that received seed among the thorns is he that heareth the word; and the care of this world, and the deceitfulness of riches, choke the word, and he becometh unfruitful.

But he that received seed into the good ground is he that heareth the word, and understandeth it; which also beareth fruit, and bringeth forth, some an hundredfold, some sixty, some thirty.

182

Matthew XIII., 3-23.

THE SOWER.

THE LEAVEN.

———

The kingdom of heaven is like unto leaven, which a woman took, and hid in three measures of meal, *till the whole was leavened.*

Matthew XIII., 33.

THE LEAVEN.

THE TARES.

The kingdom of heaven is likened unto a man which sowed good
seed in his field:

But while men slept, his enemy came and sowed tares among the
wheat, and went his way.

But when the blade was sprung up, and brought forth fruit, then
appeared the tares also.

So the servants of the householder came and said unto him, Sir,
didst not thou sow good seed in thy field? from whence then hath
it tares?

He said unto them, An enemy hath done this. The servants said
unto him, Wilt thou then that we go and gather them up?

But he said, Nay; lest while ye gather up the tares, ye root up also
the wheat with them.

Let both grow together until the harvest: and in the time of harvest
I will say to the reapers, Gather ye together first the tares, and bind
them in bundles to burn them: but gather the wheat into my barn.

Matthew XIII., 24-30.

THE TARES.

THE MUSTARD SEED.

———

The kingdom of heaven is like to a grain of mustard seed, which a man took, and sowed in his field:

Which indeed is the least of all seeds: but when it is grown, it is the greatest among herbs, and becometh a tree, so that the birds of the air come and lodge in the branches thereof.

Matthew XIII., 31-32.

———

THE HIDDEN TREASURE.

———

The kingdom of heaven is like unto treasure hid in a field; the which when a man hath found, he hideth, and for joy thereof goeth and selleth all that he hath, and buyeth that field.

Matthew XIII., 44.

THE HIDDEN TREASURE.

THE PEARL OF GREAT PRICE.

The kingdom of heaven is like unto a merchant man, seeking goodly pearls :

Who, when he had found one pearl of great price, went and sold all that he had, and bought it.

Matthew XIII., 45-46.

THE PEARL OF GREAT PRICE.

THE DRAW-NET.

———

The kingdom of heaven is like unto a net, that was cast into the sea, and gathered of every kind:

Which, when it was full, they drew to shore, and sat down, and gathered the good into vessels, but cast the bad away.

So shall it be at the end of the world: the angels shall come forth, and sever the wicked from among the just,

And shall cast them into the furnace of fire: there shall be wailing and gnashing of teeth.

Matthew XIII., 47-50.

THE UNMERCIFUL SERVANT.

———

Therefore is the kingdom of heaven likened unto a certain king, which would take account of his servants.

And when he had begun to reckon, one was brought unto him, which owed him ten thousand talents.

But forasmuch as he had not to pay, his lord commanded him to be sold, and his wife, and children, and all that he had, and payment to be made.

The servant therefore fell down and worshipped him, saying, Lord, have patience with me, and I will pay thee all.

Then the lord of that servant was moved with compassion, and loosed him, and forgave him the debt.

But the same servant went out, and found one of his fellowservants, which owed him a hundred pence: and he laid hands on him, and took him by the throat, saying, Pay me that thou owest.

And his fellowservant fell down at his feet, and besought him, saying, Have patience with me, and I will pay thee all.

And he would not: but went and cast him into prison, till he should pay the debt.

So when his fellowservants saw what was done, they were very sorry, and came and told their lord all that was done.

Then his lord, after that he had called him, said unto him, O, thou wicked servant, I forgave thee all that debt, because thou desiredst me:

Shouldest not thou also have had compassion on thy fellowservant, even as I had pity on thee?

193

THE UNMERCIFUL SERVANT.

And his lord was wroth, and delivered him to the tormentors, till he should pay all that was due unto him.

So likewise shall my heavenly Father do also unto you, if ye from your hearts forgive not every one his brother their trespasses.

Matthew XVIII., 23-35.

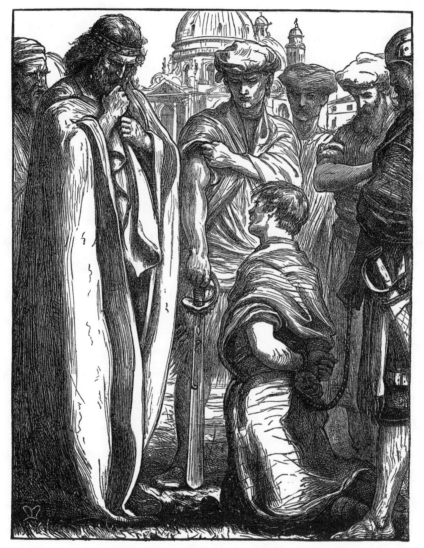

THE UNMERCIFUL SERVANT.

THE LABOURERS IN THE VINEYARD.

———

For the kingdom of heaven is like unto a man that is an house-holder, which went out early in the morning to hire labourers into his vineyard.

And when he had agreed with the labourers for a penny a day, he sent them into his vineyard.

And he went out about the third hour, and saw others standing idle in the marketplace.

And said unto them, Go ye also into the vineyard, and whatsoever is right I will give you. And they went their way.

Again he went out about the sixth and ninth hour, and did likewise.

And about the eleventh hour he went out, and found others standing idle, and saith unto them, Why stand ye here all the day idle?

They say unto him, Because no man hath hired us. He saith unto them, Go ye also into the vineyard; and whatsoever is right, that shall ye receive.

So when even was come, the lord of the vineyard saith unto his steward, Call the labourers, and give them their hire, beginning from the last unto the first.

And when they came that were hired about the eleventh hour, they received every man a penny.

But when the first came, they supposed that they should have received more; and they likewise received every man a penny.

And when they had received it, they murmured against the goodman of the house,

Saying, These last have wrought but one hour, and thou hast made them equal unto us, which have borne the burden and heat of the day.

196

THE LABOURERS IN THE VINEYARD.

THE LABOURERS IN THE VINEYARD.

But he answered one of them, and said, Friend, I do thee no wrong: didst not thou agree with me for a penny?

Take that thine is, and go thy way: I will give unto this last, even as unto thee.

Is it not lawful for me to do what I will with mine own? Is thine eye evil, because I am good?

So the last shall be first, and the first last: for many be called, but few chosen.

Matthew xx., 1-16.

THE TWO SONS.

But what think ye? A certain man had two sons; and he came to the first, and said, Son, go work to day in my vineyard.

He answered and said, I will not: but afterward he repented, and went.

And he came to the second, and said likewise. And he answered and said, I go, sir: and went not.

Whether of them twain did the will of his father? They say unto him, The first. Jesus saith unto them, Verily I say unto you, That the publicans and the harlots go into the Kingdom of God before you.

For John came unto you in the way of righteousness, and ye believed him not: but the publicans and the harlots believed him: and ye, when ye had seen it, repented not afterward, that ye might believe him.

Matthew XXI., 28-32.

THE WICKED HUSBANDMEN.

———

There was a certain householder, which planted a vineyard, and hedged it round about, and digged a winepress in it, and built a tower, and let it out to husbandmen, and went into a far country:

And when the time of the fruit drew near, he sent his servants to the husbandmen, that they might receive the fruits of it.

And the husbandmen took his servants, and beat one, and killed another, and stoned another.

Again, he sent other servants more than the first: and they did unto them likewise.

But last of all he sent unto them his son, saying, They will reverence my son.

But when the husbandmen saw the son, they said among themselves, This is the heir; come, let us kill him, and let us seize on his inheritance.

And they caught him, and cast him out of the vineyard, and slew him.

When the lord therefore of the vineyard cometh, what will he do unto those husbandmen?

They say unto him, He will miserably destroy those wicked men, and will let out his vineyard unto other husbandmen, which shall render him the fruits in their seasons.

Jesus said unto them, Did ye never read in the scriptures, The stone which the builders rejected, the same is become the head of the corner: this is the LORD's doing, and it is marvellous in our eyes?

Therefore say I unto you, The Kingdom of GOD shall be taken from you, and given to a nation bringing forth the fruits thereof.

And whosoever shall fall on this stone shall be broken: but on whomsoever it shall fall, it will grind him to powder.

Matthew XXI., 33-44.

THE WICKED HUSBANDMEN.

THE SEED GROWING SECRETLY.

———

So is the Kingdom of GOD, as if a man should cast seed into the ground;

And should sleep, and rise night and day, and the seed should spring and grow up, he knoweth not how.

For the earth bringeth forth fruit of herself; first the blade, then the ear, after that the full corn in the ear.

But when the fruit is brought forth, immediately he putteth in the sickle, because the harvest is come.

Mark IV., 26-29.

THE TEN VIRGINS.

Then shall the kingdom of heaven be likened unto ten virgins, which took their lamps, and went forth to meet the bridegroom.

And five of them were wise, and five were foolish.

They that were foolish took their lamps, and took no oil with them :

But the wise took oil in their vessels with their lamps.

While the bridegroom tarried, they all slumbered and slept.

And at midnight there was a cry made, Behold, the bridegroom cometh ; go ye out to meet him.

Then all those virgins arose, and trimmed their lamps.

And the foolish said unto the wise, Give us of your oil ; for our lamps are gone out.

But the wise answered, saying, Not so ; lest there be not enough for us and you : but go ye rather to them that sell, and buy for yourselves.

And while they went to buy, the bridegroom came ; and they that were ready went in with him to the marriage : and the door was shut.

Afterward came also the other virgins, saying, Lord, Lord, open to us.

But he answered and said, Verily I say unto you, I know you not.

Watch therefore, for ye know neither the day nor the hour wherein the Son of man cometh.

Matthew XXV., 1-13.

THE WISE AND FOOLISH VIRGINS.

THE FOOLISH VIRGINS.

THE GOOD SAMARITAN.

A certain man went down from Jerusalem to Jericho, and fell among thieves, which stripped him of his raiment, and wounded him, and departed, leaving him half dead.

And by chance there came down a certain priest that way: and when he saw him, he passed by on the other side.

And likewise a Levite, when he was at the place, came and looked on him, and passed by on the other side.

But a certain Samaritan, as he journeyed, came where he was: and when he saw him, he had compassion on him,

And went to him, and bound up his wounds, pouring in oil and wine, and set him on his own beast, and brought him to an inn, and took care of him.

And on the morrow when he departed, he took out two pence, and gave them to the host, and said unto him, Take care of him; and whatsoever thou spendest more, when I come again, I will repay thee.

Which now of these three, thinkest thou, was neighbour unto him that fell among the thieves?

And he said, He that shewed mercy on him. Then said Jesus unto him, Go, and do thou likewise.

Luke x., 30-37.

206

THE GOOD SAMARITAN.

THE FIG TREE.

Now learn a parable of the fig tree; When her branch is yet tender, and putteth forth leaves, ye know that summer is near:

So ye in like manner, when ye shall see these things come to pass, know that it is nigh, even at the doors.

Verily I say unto you, that this generation shall not pass, till all these things be done.

Heaven and earth shall pass away: but my words shall not pass away

Mark XIII., 28-31.

208

THE MERCIFUL CREDITOR.

There was a certain creditor which had two debtors: the one owed five hundred pence, and the other fifty.

And when they had nothing to pay, he frankly forgave them both. Tell me therefore, which of them will love him most?

Simon answered and said, I suppose that he to whom he forgave most. And he said unto him, Thou hast rightly judged.

And he turned to the woman, and said unto Simon, Seest thou this woman? I entered into thine house, thou gavest me no water for my feet: but she hath washed my feet with tears, and wiped them with the hairs of her head.

Thou gavest me no kiss: but this woman since the time I came in hath not ceased to kiss my feet.

My head with oil thou didst not anoint: but this woman hath anointed my feet with ointment.

Wherefore I say unto thee, Her sins, which are many, are forgiven; for she loved much: but to whom little is forgiven, the same loveth little.

Luke VII., 41-47.

209

THE IMPORTUNATE FRIEND.

———

Which of you shall have a friend, and shall go unto him at midnight, and say unto him, Friend, lend me three loaves;

For a friend of mine in his journey is come to me, and I have nothing to set before him?

And he from within shall answer and say, Trouble me not: the door is now shut, and my children are with me in bed; I cannot rise and give thee.

I say unto you, Though he will not rise and give him, because he is his friend, yet because of his importunity he will rise and give him as many as he needeth.

And I say unto you, Ask, and it shall be given you; seek, and ye shall find; knock, and it shall be opened unto you.

For every one that asketh receiveth; and he that seeketh findeth; and to him that knocketh it shall be opened.

If a son shall ask bread of any of you that is a father, will he give him a stone? or if he ask a fish, will he for a fish give him a serpent?

Or if he shall ask an egg, will he offer him a scorpion?

If ye then, being evil, know how to give good gifts unto your children: how much more shall your heavenly Father give the Holy Spirit to them that ask him?

Luke XI., 5-13.

THE IMPORTUNATE FRIEND.

THE RICH MAN.

The ground of a certain rich man brought forth plentifully:

And he thought within himself, saying, What shall I do, because I have no room where to bestow my fruits?

And he said, This will I do: I will pull down my barns, and build greater; and there will I bestow all my fruits and my goods.

And I will say to my soul, Soul, thou hast much goods laid up for many years; take thine ease, eat, drink, and be merry.

But GOD said unto him, Thou fool, this night thy soul shall be required of thee: then whose shall those things be, which thou hast provided?

So is he that layeth up treasure for himself, and is not rich toward God.

Luke XII., 16-21.

THE BARREN FIG TREE.

A certain man had a fig tree planted in his vineyard; and he came and sought fruit thereon, and found none.

Then said he unto the dresser of his vineyard, Behold, these three years I come seeking fruit on this fig tree, and find none: cut it down; why cumbereth it the ground?

And he answering said unto him, Lord, let it alone this year also, till I shall dig about it, and dung it:

And if it bear fruit, well: and if not, then after that thou shalt cut it down.

Luke XIII., 6-9.

THE MARRIAGE OF THE KING'S SON.

———

The kingdom of heaven is like unto a certain king, which made a marriage ıor his son,

And sent forth his servants to call them that were bidden to the wedding: and they would not come.

Again, he sent forth other servants, saying, Tell them which are bidden, Behold, I have prepared my dinner: my oxen and my fatlings are killed, and all things are ready: come unto the marriage.

But they made light of it, and went their ways, one to his farm, another to his merchandise:

And the remnant took his servants, and entreated them spitefully, and slew them.

But when the king heard thereof, he was wroth: and he sent forth his armies, and destroyed those murderers, and burned up their city.

Then saith he to his servants, The wedding is ready, but they which were bidden were not worthy.

Go ye therefore into the highways, and as many as ye shall find, bid to the marriage.

So those servants went out into the highways, and gathered together all as many as they found, both bad and good: and the wedding was furnished with guests.

And when the king came in to see the guests, he saw there a man which had not on a wedding garment:

And he saith unto him, Friend, how camest thou in hither not having a wedding garment? And he was speechless.

Then said the king to the servants, Bind him hand and foot, and take him away, and cast him into outer darkness: there shall be weeping and gnashing of teeth.

For many are called, but few are chosen.

Matthew XXII., 2-14.

214

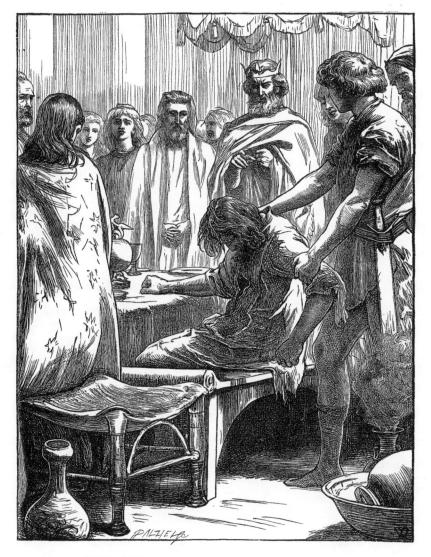

THE MARRIAGE OF THE KING'S SON.

THE FAITHFUL AND WICKED STEWARDS.

Who then is that faithful and wise steward, whom his lord shall make ruler over his household, to give them their portion of meat in due season?

Blessed is that servant, whom his lord when he cometh shall find so doing.

Of a truth I say unto you, That he will make him ruler over all that he hath.

But and if that servant say in his heart, My lord delayeth his coming; and shall begin to beat the menservants and maidens, and to eat and drink, and to be drunken;

The lord of that servant will come in a day when he looketh not for him, and at an hour when he is not aware, and will cut him in sunder, and will appoint him his portion with the unbelievers.

And that servant, which knew his lord's will, and prepared not himself, neither did according to his will, shall be beaten with many stripes.

But he that knew not, and did commit things worthy of stripes, shall be beaten with few stripes. *For unto whomsoever much is given, of him shall be much required: and to whom men have committed much, of him they will ask the more.*

Luke XII., 42-48.

THE MARRIAGE FEAST.

A certain man made a great supper, and bade many :

And sent his servant at supper time to say to them that were bidden, Come ; for all things are now ready.

And they all with one consent began to make excuse. The first said unto him, I have bought a piece of ground, and I must needs go and see it : I pray thee have me excused.

And another said, I have bought five yoke of oxen, and I go to prove them : I pray thee have me excused.

And another said, I have married a wife, and therefore I cannot come.

So that servant came, and shewed his lord these things. Then the master of the house being angry said to his servant, Go out quickly into the streets and lanes of the city, and bring in hither the poor, and the maimed, and the halt, and the blind.

And the servant said, Lord, it is done as thou hast commanded, and yet there is room.

And the lord said unto the servant, Go out into the highways and hedges, and compel them to come in, that my house may be filled.

For I say unto you, That none of those men which were bidden shall taste of my supper.

Luke XIV., 16-24.

THE LOST SHEEP.

———

What man of you, having an hundred sheep, if he lose one of them, doth not leave the ninety and nine in the wilderness, and go after that which is lost, until he find it?

And when he hath found it, he layeth it on his shoulders, rejoicing.

And when he cometh home, he calleth together his friends and neighbours, saying unto them, Rejoice with me; for I have found my sheep which was lost.

I say unto you, that likewise joy shall be in heaven over one sinner that repenteth, more than over ninety and nine just persons, which need no repentance.

Luke xv., 4-7.

THE LOST SHEEP.

THE TEN PIECES OF MONEY.

A certain nobleman went into a far country to receive for himself a kingdom, and to return.

And he called his ten servants, and delivered them ten pounds, and said unto them, Occupy till I come.

But his citizens hated him, and sent a message after him, saying, We will not have this man to reign over us.

And it came to pass, that when he was returned, having received the kingdom, then he commanded these servants to be called unto him, to whom he had given the money, that he might know how much every man had gained by trading.

Then came the first, saying, Lord, thy pound hath gained ten pounds.

And he said unto him, Well, thou good servant : because thou hast been faithful in a very little, have thou authority over ten cities.

And the second came, saying, Lord, thy pound hath gained five pounds.

And he said likewise to him, Be thou also over five cities.

And another came, saying, Lord, behold, here is thy pound, which I have kept laid up in a napkin :

For I feared thee, because thou art an austere man : thou takest up that thou layedst not down, and reapest that thou didst not sow.

And he said unto him, Out of thine own mouth will I judge thee, thou wicked servant. Thou knewest that I was an austere man, taking up that I laid not down, and reaping that I did not sow :

Wherefore then gavest not thou my money into the bank, that at my coming I might have required mine own with usury?

And he said unto them that stood by, Take from him the pound, and give it to him that hath ten pounds.

THE TEN PIECES OF MONEY.

(And they said unto him, Lord he hath ten pounds.)

For I say unto you, That unto every one which hath shall be given ; and from him that hath not, even that he hath shall be taken away from him.

But those mine enemies, which would not that I should reign over them, bring hither, and slay them before me.

Luke XIX., 12 27.

THE LOST PIECE OF SILVER.

Either what woman having ten pieces of silver, if she lose one piece, doth not light a candle, and sweep the house, and seek diligently till she find it?

And when she hath found it, she calleth her friends and her neighbours together, saying, Rejoice with me; for I have found the piece which I had lost.

Likewise, I say unto you, there is joy in the presence of the angels of God over one sinner that repenteth.

Luke xv., 8-10.

222

THE LOST PIECE OF SILVER.

THE PRODIGAL SON.

A certain man had two sons:

And the younger of them said to his father, Father, give me the portion of goods that falleth to me. And he divided unto them his living.

And not many days after the younger son gathered all together, and took his journey into a far country, and there wasted his substance with riotous living,

And when he had spent all, there arose a mighty famine in that land; and he began to be in want.

And he went and joined himself to a citizen of that country; and he sent him into his fields to feed swine.

And he would fain have filled his belly with the husks that the swine did eat; and no man gave unto him.

And when he came to himself, he said, How many hired servants of my father's have bread enough and to spare, and I perish with hunger!

I will arise and go to my father, and will say unto him, Father, I have sinned against heaven, and before thee,

And am no more worthy to be called thy son: make me as one of thy hired servants.

And he arose, and came to his father. But when he was yet a great way off, his father saw him, and had compassion, and ran, and fell on his neck, and kissed him.

And the son said unto him, Father, I have sinned against heaven, and in thy sight, and am no more worthy to be called thy son.

But the father said to his servants, Bring forth the best robe, and put it on him; and put a ring on his hand, and shoes on his feet:

And bring hither the fatted calf, and kill it; and let us eat, and be merry:

For this my son was dead, and is alive again; he was lost, and is found. And they began to be merry.

THE PRODIGAL SON.

THE PRODIGAL SON.

Now his elder son was in the field : and as he came and drew nigh to the house, he heard musick and dancing.

And he called one of the servants, and asked what these things meant.

And he said unto him, Thy brother is come ; and thy father hath killed the fatted calf, because he hath received him safe and sound.

And he was angry, and would not go in : therefore came his father out, and intreated him.

And he answering said to his father, Lo, these many years do I serve thee, neither transgressed I at any time thy commandment : and yet thou never gavest me a kid, that I might make merry with my friends :

But as soon as this thy son was come, which hath devoured thy living with harlots, thou hast killed for him the fatted calf.

And he said unto him, Son, thou art ever with me, and all that I have is thine.

It was meet that we should make merry, and be glad : for this thy brother was dead, and is alive again ; and was lost, and is found.

Luke xv., 11-32.

THE UNJUST STEWARD.

There was a certain rich man, which had a steward; and the same was accused unto him that he had wasted his goods.

And he called him, and said unto him, How is it that I hear this of thee? give an account of thy stewardship; for thou mayest be no longer steward.

Then the steward said within himself, What shall I do? for my lord taketh away from me the stewardship: I cannot dig; to beg I am ashamed.

I am resolved what to do, that, when I am put out of the stewardship, they may receive me into their houses.

So he called every one of his lord's debtors unto him, and said unto the first, How much owest thou unto my lord?

And he said, An hundred measures of oil. And he said unto him, Take thy bill, and sit down quickly, and write fifty.

Then said he to another, And how much owest thou? And he said, An hundred measures of wheat. And he said unto him, Take thy bill, and write fourscore.

And the lord commended the unjust steward, because he had done wisely: for the children of this world are in their generation wiser than the children of light.

And I say unto you, make to yourselves friends of the mammon of unrighteousness; that, when ye fail, they may receive you into everlasting habitations.

He that is faithful in that which is least, is faithful also in much: and he that is unjust in the least is unjust also in much.

If therefore ye have not been faithful in the unrighteous mammon, who will commit to your trust the true riches?

And if ye have not been faithful in that which is another man's, who shall give you that which is your own?

Luke XVI., 1-12.

THE PHARISEE AND THE PUBLICAN.

———

Two men went up into the temple to pray; the one a Pharisee, and the other a publican.

The Pharisee stood and prayed thus with himself, GOD, I thank thee, that I am not as other men are, extortioners, unjust, adulterers, or even as this publican.

I fast twice in the week, I give tithes of all that I possess.

And the publican, standing afar off would not lift up so much as his eyes unto heaven, but smote upon his breast, saying, GOD be merciful to me a sinner.

I tell you, this man went down to his house justified rather than the other;

For every one that exalteth himself shall be abased; and he that humbleth himself shall be exalted.

Luke XVIII., 10·14.

THE PHARISEE AND THE PUBLICAN.

THE RICH MAN AND LAZARUS.

There was a certain rich man, which was clothed in purple and fine linen, and fared sumptuously every day:

And there was a certain beggar named Lazarus, which was laid at his gate, full of sores,

And desiring to be fed with the crumbs which fell from the rich man's table: moreover the dogs came and licked his sores.

And it came to pass, that the beggar died, and was carried by the angels into Abraham's bosom: the rich man also died, and was buried;

And in hell he lift up his eyes, being in torments, and seeth Abraham afar off, and Lazarus in his bosom.

And he cried and said, Father Abraham, have mercy on me, and send Lazarus, that he may dip the tip of his finger in water, and cool my tongue; for I am tormented in this flame.

But Abraham said, Son, remember that thou in thy lifetime receivedst thy good things, and likewise Lazarus evil things: but now he is comforted, and thou art tormented.

And beside all this, between us and you there is a great gulf fixed: so that they which would pass from hence to you cannot; neither can they pass to us, that would come from thence.

Then he said, I pray thee therefore, father, that thou wouldest send him to my father's house:

For I have five brethren; that he may testify unto them, lest they also come into this place of torment.

Abraham saith unto him, They have Moses and the prophets; let them hear them.

And he said, Nay, father Abraham: but if one went unto them from the dead, they will repent.

And he said unto him, If they hear not Moses and the prophets, neither will they be persuaded, though one rose from the dead.

Luke XVI., 19-31.

THE RICH MAN AND LAZARUS.

THE GOOD SHEPHERD.

Verily, verily, I say unto you, He that entereth not by the door into the sheepfold, but climbeth up some other way, the same is a thief and a robber.

But he that entereth in by the door is the shepherd of the sheep.

To him the porter openeth; and the sheep hear his voice: and he calleth his own sheep by name, and leadeth them out.

And when he putteth forth his own sheep, he goeth before them, and the sheep follow him: for they know his voice.

And a stranger will they not follow, but will flee from him: for they know not the voice of strangers.

This parable spake Jesus unto them; but they understood not what things they were which he spake unto them.

Then said Jesus unto them again, Verily, verily, I say unto you, I am the door of the sheep.

All that ever came before me are thieves and robbers: but the sheep did not hear them.

I am the door: by me if any man enter in, he shall be saved, and shall go in and out, and find pasture.

The thief cometh not, but for to steal, and to kill, and to destroy: I am come that they might have life, and that they might have it more abundantly.

I am the good shepherd: the good shepherd giveth his life for the sheep.

But he that is an hireling, and not the shepherd, whose own the sheep are not, seeth the wolf coming, and leaveth the sheep, and fleeth: and the wolf catcheth them, and scattereth the sheep.

The hireling fleeth, because he is an hireling, and careth not for the sheep.

232

THE GOOD SHEPHERD.—THE HIRELING.

THE GOOD SHEPHERD.

I am the good shepherd, and know my sheep, and am known of mine.

As the Father knoweth me, even so know I the Father: and I lay down my life for the sheep.

And other sheep I have, which are not of this fold: them also I must bring, and they shall hear my voice; and there shall be one fold and one shepherd.

Therefore doth my Father love me, because I lay down my life, that I might take it again.

No man taketh it from me, but I lay it down of myself.

I have power to lay it down, and I have power to take it again. This commandment have I received of my Father.

John x , 1-18.

PERSEVERANCE.

———

For which of you, intending to build a tower, sitteth not down first, and counteth the cost, whether he have sufficient to finish it ?

Lest haply, after he hath laid the foundation, and is not able to finish it, all that behold it begin to mock him,

Saying, This man began to build, and was not able to finish.

Or what king, going to make war against another king, sitteth not down first, and consulteth whether he be able with ten thousand to meet him that cometh against him with twenty thousand ?

Or else, while the other is yet a great way off, he sendeth an embassage, and desireth conditions of peace.

So likewise, whosoever he be of you that forsaketh not all that he hath, he cannot be my disciple.

Luke XIV., 28-33.

THE UNJUST JUDGE.

There was in a city a judge, which feared not GOD, neither regarded man:

And there was a widow in that city; and she came unto him, saying, Avenge me of mine adversary.

And he would not for awhile: but afterward he said within himself, Though I fear not GOD, nor regard man;

Yet because this widow troubleth me, I will avenge her, lest by her continual coming she weary me.

And the LORD said, Hear what the unjust judge saith.

And shall not God avenge his own elect, which cry day and night unto him, though he bear long with them? I tell you that he will avenge them speedily. Nevertheless when the Son of man cometh, shall he find faith on the earth?

Luke XVIII., 2-8.

THE UNJUST JUDGE.

THE WEDDING FEAST.

When thou art bidden of any man to a wedding, sit not down in the highest room; lest a more honourable man than thou be bidden of him;

And he that bade thee and him come and say to thee, Give this man place; and thou begin with shame to take the lowest room.

But when thou art bidden, go and sit down in the lowest room; that when he that bade thee cometh, he may say unto thee, Friend, go up higher: then shalt thou have worship in the presence of them that sit at meat with thee.

For whosoever exalteth himself shall be abased; and he that humbleth himself shall be exalted.

Luke XIV., 8-11.

THE TRUE VINE.

I am the true vine, and my Father is the husbandman.

Every branch in me that beareth not fruit he taketh away: and every branch that beareth fruit, he purgeth it, that it may bring forth more fruit.

Now ye are clean through the word which I have spoken unto you.

Abide in me, and I in you. As the branch cannot bear fruit of itself, except it abide in the vine; no more can ye, except ye abide in me.

I am the vine, ye are the branches: he that abideth in me, and I in him, the same bringeth forth much fruit: for without me ye can do nothing.

If a man abide not in me, he is cast forth as a branch and is withered; and men gather them, and cast them into the fire, and they are burned.

If ye abide in me, and my words abide in you, ye shall ask what ye will, and it shall be done unto you.

Herein is my Father glorified, that ye bear much fruit; so shall ye be my disciples.

As the Father hath loved me, so have I loved you: continue ye in my love.

If ye keep my commandments, ye shall abide in my love; even as I have kept my Father's commandments, and abide in his love.

These things have I spoken unto you, that my joy might remain in you, and that your joy might be full.

This is my commandment, That ye love one another, as I have loved you.

239

THE TRUE VINE.

Greater love hath no man than this, that a man lay down his life for his friends.

Ye are my friends, if ye do whatsoever I command you.

Henceforth I call you not servants; for the servant knoweth not what his lord doeth: but I have called you friends; for all things that I have heard of my Father I have made known unto you.

Ye have not chosen me, but I have chosen you, and ordained you, that ye should go and bring forth fruit, and that your fruit should remain: that whatsoever ye shall ask of the Father in my name, he may give it you.

John xv , 1-16.